B Caruso

Greenfeld, Howard.

Caruso

CARUSO
An ILLUSTRATED LIFE

CARUSO
An ILLUSTRATED LIFE
Howard S. Greenfeld

A JULIET GARDINER BOOK

Trafalgar Square Publishing
NORTH POMFRET, VERMONT

First published in the United States of America in 1991
by Trafalgar Square Publishing
North Pomfret, Vermont 05053

Library of Congress Card Number: 91-65296

ISBN 0 943955 44 0

Typeset by Falcon Graphic Art Limited, Wallington, Surrey
Printed and bound in Great Britain by The Bath Press, Avon

General Editor Juliet Gardiner
Editors Jennifer Chilvers
Colin Ziegler
Picture Research Anna Williams
Art Director Roger Bristow
Art Editor Ruth Prentice
Designer Alison Shackleton

Title page illustration: A self-caricature
of Caruso as Canio in *Pagliacci*.

CONTENTS

PREFACE

In making the television series, 'A Tenor's Tribute', our intention was to use the singularly effective medium of television to collect and arrange the anecdotes, places, memories and atmosphere associated with the great singer, Enrico Caruso, and carry them in an entertaining way to a larger audience in the hope that they too would enjoy a portrait of a great life and an extraordinary man.

I hoped to bring my own enthusiasm for the man and the tenor to the screen and to help to explain the demands and complexities of his chosen career. Here was a man against whom all odds were heavily stacked, whose courage, perseverance and conviction turned those same odds so completely around as to make the retrospective view look as if he was simply born lucky. It was this aspect, the man himself, that I was convinced had to be the key to understanding his success. Through the many months of planning, researching and filming, this conviction was borne out. My professional admiration grew as my knowledge and understanding of the human being that fuelled his work deepened.

It is my hope that this book which tells of Caruso's life and career, will enrich your enjoyment of the programmes, 'A Tenor's Tribute', and in turn will bring you close to sharing my warmth for this giant, 'the great Caruso'.

Dennis O'Neill

AT THE AGE OF TWENTY-TWO, Caruso sang the role of Turiddu in Cavalleria Rusticana *at the Teatro Cimarosa in Caserta. It was his first appearance in a work that was part of the standard repertory. Singing with him in the role of Santuzza was Elena Bianchini-Cappelli.*

CARUSO

1
NAPLES: *The* EARLY YEARS

The via San Giovanello agli Ottocalli is like countless other congested streets that make up the working-class neighbourhoods of Naples. It was there, at number seven, in a modest second-floor apartment that Enrico (the less formal Errico was the name on the parish register) Caruso was born. The date of his birth was either 25 or 27 February 1873 — it has been celebrated on both dates. (Enrico Caruso, Jr believed that his father was born on the earlier date and that it was not registered until the 27th, but, in his words, 'No matter. He was born.')

Though this undistinguished and far from palatial building might seem an inappropriate birthplace for the man who would be known as the King of Tenors, the city of Naples itself, which played such an important role in the history of opera and song — 'the very fount and birthplace of fine singing,' Stendhal wrote — was an altogether suitable setting for such an auspicious occasion.

The birth and especially the survival of the infant at the time of a devastating cholera epidemic were as miraculous as the gift of song he would one day offer to the world, for he was the first of a large number of Caruso children — eighteen is the number usually given, though this number is certainly exaggerated — to live beyond infancy. Even under normal conditions, the rate of infant mortality was high in the disease-ridden city, and Caruso later attributed his survival in the midst of an epidemic to the aid of a wet nurse, who cared for him in place of his own mother, who was too weak to do so.

MARIA CASTALDI, a warm and intelligent woman, who married Marcellino Caruso only a few months after his wife's death, proved to be the ideal stepmother for young Enrico. The two maintained a close and loving relationship until the tenor's death.

CARUSO

Caruso's parents, who had come to Naples from a small village to the north, were far from wealthy — but they were not poor, as some legends would have it. The tenor's father, Marcellino, was known as a heavy drinker, but he was steadily employed, first as a mechanic and then as a factory superintendent, and he was always able to support his family. His wife, Anna Baldini, was a kind and gentle woman, whose health had deteriorated with the years, but who lavished on her first healthy child her quiet strength and profound affection.

Enrico, a good-natured boy, returned this affection; he was uncommonly devoted to his mother. In the absence of his father, who preferred to spend most of his evenings at local cafés, Enrico undertook, at a very early age, many of the responsibilities of the household, responsibilities far more suited to a boy twice his age. He was a normally playful and noisy child, but he already showed a sense of duty that would characterize him throughout his life.

His playground was the colourful Neapolitan waterfront, where the teeming, overcrowded city came to life. There he learned to swim and dive, and, like so many boys who lived near the harbour, he dreamt of being a sailor.

But his parents had other plans for him. His mother, who had taught him to read, wanted him to have a formal education; his father disagreed, he was determined to apprentice him to a mechanical engineer. A compromise was reached: at the age of ten the boy was sent to work as an apprentice, but he was also allowed to attend classes at the Bronzini Institute, which specialized in training young boys to sing in local church choirs.

His job bored him, as did his regular studies at school, but his singing classes delighted him. 'It was as natural for me to sing as it was to play,' he wrote many years later. And he was appreciated by his teachers, who discovered that the new student had an extraordinarily fine contralto voice, so fine a voice that he soon became the principal soloist of the school's choir, known throughout Naples for its excellence and much sought after by churches for use in their services and religious processions.

In spite of his successes as a singer, however, it was obvious that the boy would never become a good student, and his father, vindicated, demanded that he give up his studies and work regular hours at his job. He would be allowed to sing all he wanted, but only after a full day's work which might prepare him for a serious future.

MARCELLINO CARUSO, the tenor's father, enjoyed drinking at local cafés, but he worked hard and never failed to support his family. As far as he was concerned, his son's musical education was a waste of time.

Enrico had no choice but to give in to his father's wishes, but he had no intention of giving up singing. He was frequently called upon to offer serenades to young ladies, on behalf of their unmusical fiancés, and occasionally he offered his services at social functions. In addition, he continued to sing at church services whenever he had the opportunity.

One such religious service, on 1 June 1888, marked the saddest day in the young boy's life. On that morning, he had been asked to sing at the Church of San Severino as part of the celebration of Corpus Christi. He especially loved singing at these services, but this time the fifteen-year-old boy hesitated: his mother was very ill, and he was torn between his obligation to sing at the church and his desire to stay by her side and give her comfort.

At his mother's insistence, he set off for the church. In the middle of the service, there was an interruption. Neighbours, who had seen Marcellino Caruso emerge weeping from his home, had come to the church to tell young Enrico that his mother had died. It was a terrible moment — Enrico had been very close to his mother, and it was her faith that encouraged him to go on singing. But it was also, in a way, a liberating moment, since he had worked at the factory largely to help to support his mother and would now be free to do just what he wanted — to please himself and only himself. To fail at music, which was of course a possibility, seemed to him far more honourable than to succeed at his tedious work at the factory.

He had to be patient, however. His strong contralto voice was changing, and during that period he feared that his singing voice might never return; this was the fate of many promising boy sopranos. In addition, his responsibilities at home towards his younger brother and sister — Giovanni, born in 1876, and Assunta, born in 1882 — were, for a while, greater than ever. He had to replace his mother in as many ways as he could.

Fortunately, this responsibility was of short duration, for, only five and a half months after the death of Anna, Marcellino remarried, and his second wife, Maria Castaldi, took charge of the home and the children with intelligence and kindness. But the problem of his singing voice remained, and while, for two years, Enrico marked time at his job, he continued to worry that he would lose his ability to sing. He never gave up, however, and, though

ANNA BALDINI CARUSO, the tenor's beloved mother, who encouraged her son to continue his studies. This photograph is taken from a pastel which Caruso kept at his bedside.

his musical activities were necessarily curtailed as his voice changed and developed, he managed to sing whenever the opportunity was presented to him. His perseverance was rewarded, as it became increasingly obvious that the boy with the sweet contralto voice was becoming a man with an equally pleasing voice somewhere between tenor and baritone. Even his father had reluctantly come to realize that his eldest son's future lay beyond the confines of the factory and that he was determined to pursue his dream of becoming a singer.

NAPLES IN 1900, with its magnificent bay and Mount Vesuvius looming in the background. It was here that Caruso was born and here that he died.

The first concrete steps in this direction were taken in the summer of 1890, when Enrico was seventeen years old. Naples, his home, was at the time one of the liveliest and most enchanting cities of Europe. Rising above and enclosing a magnificent bay, dominated by the imposing sight of the ever-threatening Mount Vesuvius, and animated by its vigorous and passionate people — both ingratiating and infuriating — it drew visitors from every part of the world. The rebirth in the 1880s of the Neapolitan song — haunting, melodious expressions of the population's joys and sorrows — added enormously to the city's charms and gave rise to an immensely popular form of entertainment known as the *café-chantant* — the singing café. Neapolitan songs, accompanied by guitar, mandolin, or piano, were sung throughout the city, but nowhere more effectively than in these cafés which lined the city's colourful harbour.

It was these cafés that Caruso visited during the summer of 1890 — to learn from the expert singers of Neapolitan melodies and, whenever possible, to become part of the entertainment himself. He earned very little money that first summer, but his sweet voice was noticed, even attracting the attention of one client who offered to send him to his brother for singing lessons. (Caruso accepted the generous offer, but after eleven lessons he came to the conclusion that the lessons were doing him more harm than good.)

The following summer, a more promising opportunity presented itself when the owner of a well-known café, the Risorgimento at the rotunda of the via Caracciolo, which ran along the crescent of the bay, suggested that the young man join the regular entertainers at his café. He would not only have a chance to sing before an audience; he would also be allowed to keep whatever money the customers cared to give him.

Caruso enthusiastically agreed to the arrangement, and each evening, after a day's work as a mechanic, he would go to the Risorgimento, often receiving nothing for his troubles, but occasionally earning a few lire. By the end of the summer, he had earned more than money; he had earned the enduring friendship of Eduardo Missiano, a young baritone whose interest in his talent radically changed young Caruso's life. Missiano, the son of a wealthy Neapolitan family, had never sung in public — he had apparently more taste than talent — but he was studying with one of the city's most distinguished teachers, Guglielmo Vergine, and he offered to take Caruso to Vergine to arrange for lessons. It was, obviously, an offer the young man could not refuse, a chance to study voice professionally for the very first time.

At their first meeting Vergine was unimpressed, complaining that Caruso's voice sounded like 'the wind whistling through a window', but at a second audition he reluctantly — with Missiano's urging — agreed to teach the inexperienced tenor.

It was an opportunity Caruso had eagerly sought, but he knew it would be difficult. In addition to studying with Vergine, he had to continue his work at the factory and he had to continue, whenever possible, singing at the waterfront cafés. But the young man persevered; he was as energetic and tireless as he was ambitious to become a singer. He had had no formal musical education, and he

ASSUNTA CARUSO, born in 1882, was Enrico's only sister. The two were not close and saw little of each other after the tenor left Naples. She died in 1915.

did not receive one — in the traditional sense — from Vergine, but he had an innate musical sense, had been gifted with perfect pitch, and was able to absorb quickly and intelligently the lessons of his unsmiling, demanding teacher. Vergine was the first to train him in the art of singing, and succeeded in turning him into a true tenor by teaching him how to use his voice. Caruso, though not encouraged by his teacher at the beginning of his career, never failed to give him credit for his later success.

CARUSO, on the right, and two men who played important roles during his first years as a singer. Enrico Pignataro, a baritone, who sang with him in Caserta in 1895 and found him work at the Teatro Bellini in Naples a few months later, is on the left; and Guglielmo Vergine, his first professional singing teacher, is in the centre.

In February 1894, Caruso celebrated his twenty-first birthday. His years of study had served him well; even Vergine agreed that he was ready to make his operatic début in one of the lesser Neapolitan theatres or in a nearby provincial opera house. (At the time, even small, provincial towns could boast opera seasons.) However, a

twenty-first birthday meant more than a coming of age for an Italian male: it meant that the time had come for him to serve his three years of military service.

Caruso, who had hoped that he might be rejected because of his none too sturdy physique, was no exception, and, shortly after his birthday, he was called up and ordered to join the Thirteenth Artillery at Rieti. During the trip to the army camp, some fifty miles from Rome, he was disconsolate. He knew that three years without singing at this crucial stage could well mean the end of his career, that all of his years of dedication might have been wasted. And they might well have been had it not been for his meeting at Rieti with an army major who, almost miraculously, appreciated his talents.

As a soldier, Caruso was predictably inept. He performed his duties perfunctorily, and in his free time he sang. He sang in an effort to improve his voice and for the sheer joy of singing, as well as for the pleasure his singing seemed to give his fellow soldiers. Only the commanding officer, Major Nagliati, was not entertained. Complaining that the young man's voice was disturbing his own work as well as the camp's routine, he angrily summoned Caruso to his office where he questioned him sharply, and, most surprisingly, revealed himself to be a knowledgeable music-lover. Caruso, he realized, was a serious musician, and to confirm his own feelings that the young Neapolitan might be of more use to his country as a singer than as a soldier, he arranged an introduction to one of Rieti's noblemen, the Baron Costa, himself an accomplished musician. The baron agreed that the young man was indeed gifted — extraordinarily so, in his opinion. He took Caruso in hand, offered him his home as a practice studio, accompanied him on the piano, and coached him. In only five days — an astoundingly short time — he managed to teach him the demanding role of Turiddu in Mascagni's *Cavalleria Rusticana* — the first complete role Caruso had ever learned.

There were no longer any doubts on the part of the major or the baron. Deeply impressed by the young soldier's talent, they agreed that it would be a waste to keep him in the service, and they found a solution. After less than two months, Enrico Caruso was discharged from the army. He was, it was claimed, needed at home to support his family, and his younger brother Giovanni was called up to replace him.

2
The
BEGINNING
of a CAREER

Caruso, again a civilian, arrived in Naples on Easter Sunday, more determined than ever to make a place for himself in the world of opera — no matter how great the sacrifice. As a first step, he decided not to return to his job at the factory; the money he could make there could not compensate for the time lost in the pursuit of his career. Instead he would have to manage to live on the meagre earnings from his occasional appearances at church festivities and at the city's waterfront cafés.

He resumed his studies with Vergine, with increased energy, able to devote far more time to them than he had in the past. Vergine's attitude towards his pupil had changed. No longer belittling him, he showered the young tenor with praise and took an active and enthusiastic part in trying to further his professional career, arranging auditions for him whenever possible.

The most promising of these was held in the autumn of 1894 before Nicola Daspuro, a well-known newspaperman, who had been asked by the great Milanese publishing firm of Sonzogno to organize a season of opera at the Mercadante, one of Naples' most illustrious theatres. Among his many talents, Daspuro was a competent musician and sometime librettist, who acted as Sonzogno's representative for southern Italy. His first season as impresario at the newly remodelled Mercadante had been enormously successful, and as a result he was besieged by singing teachers from far and wide, eager to place their pupils in his company. Among these was Vergine, whom Daspuro had known for years and whose opinion he trusted. Although Daspuro assured him that no matter how good Caruso was, there was no room in his company for an additional singer, Vergine continued to plead the young tenor's case, and Daspuro finally agreed to give him an audition.

Given Caruso's lack of experience, the audition was surprisingly successful, and the impresario was sufficiently impressed to promise to try to give him a part at some time during the forthcoming season. A few days later, the company's conductor, Giovanni Zuccani, listened to Caruso and agreed with Daspuro's judgement: it was decided that the young tenor should study the role of Wilhelm Meister in the French opera *Mignon*, which would serve as his début.

That début never took place. When Caruso, together with the other singers — all of them experienced professionals — was called to the piano rehearsals, he seemed a changed man. Almost completely paralysed with fear, he did everything wrong: he forgot his lines, he missed his cues, and he sang out of tune. Zuccani, a kindly man, tried to calm him, but it was useless. Finally, no longer able to continue the rehearsal, the conductor rose from the piano, turned to Vergine, and said, 'Tell him yourself that it is impossible to present him on stage in such a state.' Vergine, his eyes filled with tears, lowered his head, and, without comment, led the distraught young singer away.

It was a humiliating experience for young Caruso, but within a few months he got another chance, one of far less artistic importance, but one that did enable him to make his first professional appearance as an opera singer.

A wealthy young composer named Domenico Morelli had hired a theatre, the Teatro Nuovo, and was recruiting a company to perform his first opera, *L'Amico Francesco*. At the suggestion of a musician who had appeared with Caruso at a number of church festivities, he offered the twenty-one-year-old tenor the role of the fifty-year-old protagonist. (The baritone who was to sing the role of Caruso's adopted son was nearly sixty years old!)

Caruso had almost two months to study his part, and all went well until the night of the dress rehearsal, when the tenor realized he had neither the shoes, the stockings nor the scarf needed for his role. Morelli and the director were furious, and angrily asked the young

A YOUNG CARUSO in Rigoletto, *as he appeared in the role of the Duke at Naples' Teatro Mercadante in 1896. It was an enormously successful season for the twenty-three-year-old tenor, and during it he sang in ten performances of Verdi's masterpiece.*

[Mishkin Studio, New York

Signor ENRICO CARUSO

man why he had not bought the appropriate costume with the money they had paid in advance for his four performances. Caruso's explanation — that the money paid would barely cover the cost of the four meals he would have to buy before the performances — was accepted, and Morelli himself sent out for the articles of clothing, allowing the rehearsal to continue successfully.

The opera itself, however, was far from successful, and the date of 15 March 1895 will be remembered as the date on which Caruso made his operatic début, and not as the date of the first performance of *L'Amico Francesco*, which was given only two of its scheduled four performances.

All was not lost, however. In spite of the opera's dismal failure, Caruso's appearance in it enabled him to be heard by two men who would be of help to him at this early stage of his career. One was Francesco Zucchi, an elderly theatrical agent who supplied singers to provincial opera houses; and the other was Carlo Ferrara, the impresario of one such theatre, the Cimarosa, in the nearby town of Caserta, who agreed to hire Caruso for his next season.

That season began less than two weeks after Caruso's last performance in *L'Amico Francesco*, and proved disastrous. Caruso was criticized for both his singing and his acting, and he returned to Naples penniless — business at the box office had been as poor as were the tenor's reviews. Yet something had been gained from that short, four-week season: the young tenor had for the first time sung two roles — in *Faust* and in *Cavalleria Rusticana* — that were part of the standard repertory, and he had demonstrated that he could master these with surprising speed. And, once again, an unsuccessful experience led to another engagement, this time in Naples itself.

The engagement was at the Teatro Bellini, one of the city's most distinguished opera houses. Shortly after Caruso's return home from Caserta, the leading tenor at the Bellini fell ill, and a substitute was urgently needed. Enrico Pignataro, a baritone who had sung with Caruso at Caserta, suggested that the young tenor would be the ideal replacement, and the theatre's desperate impresario immediately went out in search of him. He found him playing cards at a small neighbourhood café, and, to the young man's amazement offered him twenty-five lire to sing in *Faust* a few days later. Since Caruso had never before been offered such a large sum, and since he was already familiar with the role, he accepted enthusiastically.

OF ALL HIS MANY ROLES, Caruso was most closely identified with that of the strolling player, Canio, in Leoncavallo's Pagliacci. *He first sang it, substituting for an indisposed tenor, in November 1896 in Salerno. Yet it was not, as was often reported, his favourite role. 'I have no favourite roles at all,' he told a journalist. 'It is all work, all a part of my business. . .'*

A 1900 PHOTOGRAPH of the Teatro Comunale in Salerno. Caruso sang there in 1896 and at his début 'earned the whole-hearted admiration of the public with his firm and beautiful voice', according to La Gazzetta Musicale di Milano. *During that season, he met a vocal coach, Vincenzo Lombardi, who helped him to expand his vocal range and whose training proved to be invaluable.*

His performance, only a few nights later, went well. Only months after the fiasco of *L'Amico Francesco*, he was, for the very first time, singled out for praise by a critic who wrote prophetically in *Il Mattino* that 'Caruso has a beautiful voice, and if he is willing to develop it with perseverance, it will bring him great profit . . .'

The young tenor continued to sing at the Bellini for the rest of the season — adding roles in *Rigoletto* and *La Traviata* to his repertoire. His reviews were not always good, but his sweet, fresh voice pleased the public, and at the end of the season he was asked to sing again at the Bellini the following autumn. This offer of a subsequent engagement was the tenor's first assurance that he could earn a steady, if modest, income from his singing. Equally encouraging was yet another offer, to perform for the first time outside Italy.

Word of Caruso's achievements at the Bellini had reached Adolfo Bracale, a young Italian cellist with the orchestra of the Khedival Theatre — Egypt's leading opera house. Bracale wanted to start his own opera company of Italian singers whom he would present to audiences throughout Egypt. He had heard of Caruso from a friend in Naples, and on the basis of his enthusiastic reports was led to believe that the inexperienced tenor might well become the star of his new company.

Bracale was not disappointed when, after arriving in Naples, he met and listened to Caruso for the first time. The young man was obviously inexperienced, and his range was — as others had noted — somewhat limited, but Bracale was profoundly impressed with his phrasing, his tonal quality and the timbre of his voice. Agreeing to pay him more than the tenor had ever been paid before, Bracale engaged him.

The gamble paid off, and Caruso was a great success wherever he sang. He gave one bad performance — he had not yet understood the perils of too much wine — but he soon made up for it and was enthusiastically acclaimed in both Alexandria and Cairo. By the time he embarked on the voyage home, he had sung two new roles, in *La Gioconda* and in *Manon Lescaut*, and had enjoyed his first triumphs before a foreign public. The public was not a very sophisticated one — it was, in fact, made up in large part of Italian immigrants — but the young man had demonstrated his ability to bring an audience to its feet, and that alone was a considerable achievement. What he needed now were further opportunities to sing before the public. Not yet a polished artist, and without the advantage of years of formal musical education, he could only develop his natural gifts through experience on the stage.

Because of this, it was especially heartening for Caruso to learn upon his return to Naples that he had been offered a contract to sing at the Teatro Mercadante (the scene, not so long ago, of his disastrous audition) in late November — following the few appearances at the Bellini which had already been scheduled. The Mercadante was an important opera house. Though its company was not as distinguished as it had been the previous year under Daspuro, who had moved on, it drew intelligent, knowledgeable audiences and received considerable attention from the press, not only in Naples but throughout Italy.

The decision to hire Caruso had evidently been made at the last moment, for there was no advance announcement of his engagement and no pre-season publicity of any kind. Nonetheless, his season was an extraordinarily active one; in less than three months he sang in fifty performances, including one new role, in Bellini's *Romeo e Giulietta*. Sometimes he sang twice a day, and over a period of eight days — between Christmas and New Year's Day — he sang nine times. In spite of this enormous amount of activity — evidence of his energy and stamina — he never failed to acquit himself with honour. It was not long before critics took note of what they recognized to be his unusual gifts, predicting for him a brilliant future.

It was not only the critics who recognized the tenor's natural gifts. The great French soprano, Emma Calvé heard him sing during that season at the Mercadante and remembered in her autobiography that she was 'overcome with astonishment' upon hearing that 'marvellous, extraordinary voice . . . a miracle'.

The tenor's progress had been remarkable — he had made his first appearance on any stage less than a year before — and his popularity was such that at the end of January 1896, a special performance of *Faust* was given in his honour at the Mercadante. Such *serate d'onore* were not uncommon in Italian theatres at the time, but they did signify the recognition of a singer's achievements in the course of a season. In the case of a young, inexperienced tenor, these achievements were of special significance, for they guaranteed him contracts for future engagements at both the Bellini and the Mercadante, which meant opportunities to develop his art more fully.

They also led to an important engagement at nearby Salerno, beginning the following June. There, for the first time, he was able to establish that extraordinary personal rapport with his public — a rapport which marked his entire career and would make him more than just a great singer. The people of Salerno cheered Caruso's performances loudly, and they also delighted in his behaviour away from the theatre. Witty, good-humoured, and light-hearted, he was offered invitations from the town's leading citizens, sharing their meals and ingratiating himself by singing arias and songs whenever requested. By the end of that first season, he had become a local hero, and opera goers eagerly looked forward to his return, as a man and as a singer.

Equally impressed with the young tenor and eager for his return to Salerno was the conductor Vincenzo Lombardi. Lombardi was not merely a conductor, he was also a distinguished vocal coach who had worked with Calvé, as well as with the great master of *bel canto* and the reigning favourite of Neapolitan audiences, the tenor Fernando de Lucia. He summoned Caruso to his studio and asked him to sing the role of Arturo in Bellini's *I Puritani*, which he planned to perform the following

A POSTER *announcing a performance of* La Gioconda, *given in Caruso's honour at the Teatro Municipale in Salerno on 30 April 1897. Note the use of 'Errico' as the tenor's first name.*

CARUSO AS ENZO in Ponchielli's La Gioconda. *He first sang the role in Egypt in 1895, during his first operatic season outside Italy.*

August and September. At first, Caruso declined, explaining that his difficulties in the upper register would prevent him from singing the role. However, with the promise of Lombardi's help as a vocal coach, he agreed to sing not only *I Puritani*, but also *Cavalleria Rusticana* in Salerno.

Lombardi's training was invaluable. 'He got me to put more power behind my tones,' Caruso explained to his first biographer, Pierre Key, 'and although I did not, until much later, get the top notes as I should, I was finally able, through his instruction, to give all those in the *Puritani* music which the tenor must sing.' As a result, Caruso's performances in the Bellini opera were even more successful than were his appearances in the less spectacular *Cavalleria Rusticana*. He was even praised by the great De Lucia himself, who personally congratulated Caruso, already mentioned as his potential successor, while advising him to continue his studies.

Another admirer, and an influential one at this point in his career, was Giuseppe Grassi, the owner of a powerful local newspaper as well as the official impresario of Salerno's Teatro Comunale. Grassi's enthusiasm for Caruso was so great that he proposed a special Caruso season for the following October and November, an offer Caruso accepted enthusiastically, not only for the honour, but also because it would permit him more time to study with Lombardi, who was making slow, if steady, progress towards extending the tenor's range. It was another enormously successful season; its highlight, Caruso's first appearance as Canio in *Pagliacci*, was an unscheduled appearance, since the tenor substituted at the last moment for an indisposed singer. It was a role the tenor had only recently learned, one which he would make his own, and it earned him a thunderous ovation the first time, as it would throughout his career.

Caruso left Salerno in triumph, promising to return there for a longer season the following March. His place in the hearts of the citizens of Salerno was secure, and he had also won the heart of Giuseppina Grassi, the impresario's daughter, whom he rather impetuously promised to marry. The seaside town, thirty miles from Naples, had brought him every honour — professional and apparently personal — to which he had aspired.

His progress as a singer and as a musician was obvious to all who heard him, especially to his first teacher, Vergine. It was to Vergine's advantage to help the young tenor as much as he could since Caruso had agreed to give his teacher a large percentage of his future earnings instead of monetary payments (which he was unable to make) for his lessons. He felt his pupil had matured sufficiently to warrant another audition with Daspuro, whom he persuaded to attend a performance Caruso gave in Salerno. Vergine was right. This time, Sonzogno's representative was convinced of the young tenor's ability. He found his voice to be 'full, warm, and vibrant with passion', and promised to do what he could to have him engaged for a series of performances at the Teatro Lirico in Milan.

Daspuro more than kept his word. He not only arranged for Caruso's début in Milan, the operatic capital of Italy, but he also convinced the impresario of Palermo's Teatro Massimo to sign him for an engagement at the important Sicilian theatre immediately following his last performance in Salerno. Shortly afterwards, he left the

CARUSO

city in which he had had his greatest success, no longer engaged to Signorina Grassi (whose father had already made plans for their wedding), but in the company of a new love, one of the twelve ballerinas who had performed the 'Dance of the Hours' in *La Gioconda*.

When he arrived in Palermo in May 1897, Caruso was in high spirits. At the age of twenty-four, he was about to make his début at one of Europe's most important opera houses — at the time, the stage of the Massimo was the second largest on the Continent, surpassed only by that of the Paris Opéra — and a début in Milan had been arranged for the autumn. He was carefree, optimistic, and in love, and he approached his Palermo début with youthful self-confidence.

That self-confidence, however, was soon shattered when, at the very first rehearsal of *La Gioconda*, the opera which was to open the season, it became apparent that it would be difficult, if not impossible, for the young tenor to win the approval of the conductor, Leopoldo Mugnone, a fellow Neapolitan and one of Italy's most esteemed musicians. The conductor was cold at his first meeting with the tenor and relentlessly critical throughout the rehearsals. His attitude was difficult to explain. There were rumours that Mugnone was in love with the same young ballerina who had demonstrated her preference for Caruso; and there was more serious talk that the conductor was dismayed by Caruso's inability to reach the high notes of Ponchielli's score. Whatever the reason, he constantly expressed his dissatisfaction, wondering aloud if the tenor could ever master the role.

On the night of the public dress rehearsal, however, Mugnone finally succumbed to Caruso's natural gifts, spontaneously calling 'bravo' at the tenor's performance. It was the unexpected beginning of a warm friendship — and the ballerina, apparently, was forgotten by both of them. Curiously, Caruso also experienced initial difficulties in winning over the public at the Massimo. At his first appearance there — it was an historic event, part of the 2,500-seat theatre's inaugural programme — he was greeted coldly by an audience which believed that the honour of singing on such a gala occasion should have gone to a Sicilian tenor. But in subsequent performances, he won the respect and affection of the reticent public, who agreed with the critic for the influential *Giornale di Sicilia* that 'a splendid future awaits the young artist'.

CARUSO

3
His FIRST SUCCESSES

T he season in Palermo marked a turning point in Caruso's career. Having been acclaimed by a discriminating audience of sophisticated music lovers at the Massimo, he could no longer be considered merely 'promising'. Though he was not exactly deluged with offers yet, he could be certain that his success with the critics and the public, as well as his newly established contacts, would result in being offered many opportunities to sing.

While awaiting his eagerly anticipated début in Milan, he accepted one such offer, to give a number of performances in the Tuscan seaport of Livorno. The operas he was asked to sing were *La Traviata* and Puccini's *La Bohème*. *La Traviata* presented no problems, but before he could sing *La Bohème*, Caruso had a formidable obstacle to overcome. Puccini's latest opera, though only moderately successful at its première in February 1896, had in a very short time achieved enormous success with the public wherever it was performed. As a result, *La Bohème*'s publisher, Ricordi, guarded his valuable property jealously and carefully watched over each production of the opera. Special importance was attached to the new production to be given in Livorno, because it was only an hour from the composer's home at Torre del Lago, and the casting of each role had to be approved by the publisher. The cast selected by the producer was well-known — with one exception, Caruso, whose relative inexperience made him unlikely to be accepted by Ricordi.

CARUSO AS RODOLFO in Puccini's La Bohème. *He sang the role with two superb Mimis — Nellie Melba and Geraldine Farrar — but the most important Mimi of his life was Ada Giachetti, with whom he sang in Livorno in 1897 and with whom he lived for many years.*

CARUSO

There was only one possible solution: if Caruso could audition before the composer and obtain his approval, Ricordi would consent to his singing in *La Bohème*. So, Caruso travelled the short distance to Puccini's lakeside villa. Having studied the role carefully, he approached the composer confidently and sang for him Rodolfo's first-act aria. Puccini was deeply moved and, according to legend, turned to Caruso and asked, 'Who sent you to me — God?' Inviting the young tenor to spend a few hours with him, he assured Caruso that he would express his approval to Ricordi the next day.

Caruso's first appearance in *La Bohème*, in the presence of the composer who had coached him in the role, was immensely successful. Throughout his season in Livorno, the two men met often; it was the beginning of a long and mutually rewarding friendship, both professionally and personally.

Another meeting was of even greater importance to Caruso during this short season in Livorno. He and Ada Giachetti-Botti, the soprano who had sung Mimi to his Rodolfo, had fallen in love. Caruso had been in love before, but this time the involvement was a serious one. Though several years older than he was, and married (she was separated from her husband, Botti), Giachetti was an ideal partner for the young tenor. A very attractive woman, strong-willed and intelligent, she was a competent if undistinguished soprano. But she was a trained musician and an energetic teacher, and her wisdom and experience were of great help to the unschooled Caruso. Giachetti studied roles with him, helped him to develop his voice, and taught him the elements of acting. Deeply in love with him, her devotion during their early years together gave Caruso courage during his difficult times and the wisdom to cope with the fame that came to him so quickly.

Following his last performance in Livorno, however, Caruso was concerned not with fame but with the need to sustain himself until the time of his autumn engagement in Milan. To get to the city, he had to borrow money from friends in Florence; to remain in the thriving metropolis, he had to ask for an advance against his salary at the Lirico.

When he had signed a contract to sing at the prestigious theatre several months earlier, his assignment had been vague. He was asked to study three different roles, one of which would be chosen for his début. Five days before that scheduled début, he was called to the theatre

CARUSO

and told that instead of the three operas he had studied so diligently, he was to sing in another one, Jules Massenet's *La Navarraise*, an opera he had never heard. He was stunned. His protests that he could not possibly learn the role, admittedly a short one, in so little time were ignored, and he was ordered to begin work at once.

It was a nearly impossible task, but Caruso persevered, and, in spite of a disastrous dress rehearsal, he sang so brilliantly at his first performance that one influential critic singled him out for praise, affirming that he was 'on the path to a brilliant career'.

These were heartening words, and the young tenor gave further proof of his artistry in subsequent performances of two minor operas as well as in his first Milan appearance in *Cavalleria Rusticana*. Nevertheless, his greatest success of the season came at the world première of Francesco Cilea's *L'Arlesiana*. This first performance of a new opera by a promising composer had been eagerly awaited, but the work was greeted without enthusiasm from the very beginning, as was the singing of the soprano in the title role. Indeed, the public remained unmoved until Caruso, in the role of a young farmer, concluded his aria, *É la solita storia*. Suddenly the new opera came to life. Cheers rang throughout the theatre, and the tenor was forced to repeat the aria twice; at the end of the evening, an ecstatic audience called him before the curtain twenty times. The new opera had failed, but Caruso himself had achieved a great personal triumph, in the most important test of his short career.

Each time Caruso appeared, he was acclaimed, and by the time his season ended — with a performance of *Pagliacci* — his popularity had exceeded all expectations. He had even won the praise of the brilliant dramatic tenor, Francesco Tamagno, who predicted that 'he will be greater than all of us.' Caruso was not yet the equal of Tamagno nor of De Lucia or Jean de Reszke, the elegant Polish tenor, but he was already well established in the world of opera, and a bright future seemed certain. He enjoyed his operatic successes thoroughly, just as he found great pleasure in his personal life. Giachetti had encouraged him and given him a sense of security; she stood loyally by his side whenever her own commitments permitted. And on 2 July 1898, they became the parents of a son, whom they named Rodolfo (Fofò) in honour of their meeting while performing together in *La Bohème*.

ADA GIACHETTI, the mother of the tenor's two sons, lived with Caruso from 1897 to 1908, when she left him for the family chauffeur. She remained, according to his friends, the great love of Caruso's life.

Caruso's professional successes continued — in Genoa, in Fiume, in Trento, and at the Lirico. But his greatest triumph to date was 17 November 1898; this was the night he became a star. The occasion was the world première of *Fedora*, the latest opera by Umberto Giordano, who had won fame two years earlier with his rousing *Andrea Chénier*. Giordano had written the tenor role of Loris for his friend Roberto Stagno, but only a few months before the opera was to be given its first performance Stagno died suddenly of a heart attack. In desperation, and with misgivings on the part of the composer, Caruso, who was still relatively inexperienced, was offered the role.

On the night of the première, the Lirico was filled to capacity; it was an occasion of major importance in the world of opera. Cilea and Leoncavallo, Giordano's rivals, were there, as was the young conductor, Arturo Toscanini. Critics came from all over Italy, as well as from abroad.

The evening began badly. The composer, who himself conducted the opera, was greeted with no more than polite applause. The soprano was also welcomed without enthusiasm, and after the first act there were but two curtain calls. All seemed lost until the second act when Caruso stepped forward to sing his short, passionate aria, 'Amor ti vieta'. When he reached the end, the audience rose to its feet in a spontaneous outburst, which could not be stopped until the aria was repeated. Even then, the applause was deafening, and the performance almost had to be halted. The tenor's delivery of this one aria, had overwhelmed the public and transformed a disappointing evening into a rousing success. He sang, one critic noted, 'as one of the good Lord's creatures in that happy land can — with the sun and the sky and the stars of the perfumed night in his voice expressing the ever-new marvels of the everlasting universal life'.

Following his performance that night, the tenor's future was secure. 'Caruso sang in *Fedora*', it was said, and *'la fé d'oro'* (made it golden). It could equally be said that the new role, which suited his voice so perfectly that it might have been written for him, made Caruso, golden. Word of his extraordinary triumph spread throughout Europe and even to America. In the tenor's own words, 'Contracts descended on me like a heavy rainstorm.'

4
The
INTERNATIONAL STAR

T he year 1899 marked the emergence of Caruso as an international star. In the course of that year, he would sing for the first time in Rome and also establish himself as a favourite in two of the musical capitals of the world — St Petersburg and Buenos Aires.

He left for Russia shortly after the end of his season at the Lirico. His appearances in St Petersburg would constitute his most formidable challenge to date, and when he left Italy he did so with a mixture of apprehension and self-confidence. The Russian metropolis, unlike Cairo and Alexandria, was a thriving, culturally sophisticated city, with an opera-loving public accustomed to the very best. The company with which Caruso would be singing was also an outstanding one of seasoned professionals. From the very beginning, it was obvious that he was perfectly at home with such a group. One of them, Luisa Tetrazzini, who sang Musetta to Caruso's Rodolfo in St Petersburg, spoke to Fred Gaisberg, a pioneer of the recording industry, of the tenor's progress at this time:

> I remember Enrico as a youth of twenty, years before his voice was yet rounded and the different registers smoothed out. I recall the difficulty he had even with such ordinary notes as G or A. He always stumbled over these and it annoyed him so that he even threatened to change over to a baritone voice.

Several years later, when she sang *La Bohème* with him in St Petersburg, she was astounded at the change.

THE ROLE OF RADAMES in Aida *became one of Caruso's favourites. He first sang it in St Petersburg on 18 December 1899. 'Much of the growth I gained at that time I attributed to the singing of Radames,' he said later. 'It developed and consolidated my voice.'*

35

I can hear that velvet voice now, and the *impertinenza* with which he lavishly poured forth those rich, round notes. It was the open *voce napoletana* (Neapolitan voice), yet it had the soft caress of the *voce della campagna toscana* (voice of the Tuscan countryside). There was never any doubt in my mind. I placed him then and there as an extraordinary and unique tenor. From top to bottom his register was without defect.

The Russian audiences agreed, and cheered the tenor enthusiastically each time he sang. This acclaim gave the young tenor even greater self-confidence. Secure artistically (as well as financially), he was able to enjoy himself as he wandered among unfamiliar sights and unfamiliar people, joking with his illustrious colleagues with whom he now felt completely at ease. He was suddenly famous, and he thoroughly enjoyed his fame. In St Petersburg, too, he took part in his first command performance before royalty at the fabulous palace of Tsar Nicolas II. It was a splendid occasion which he never forgot.

A triumphant Caruso returned to Milan in high spirits. Once again, he sang in *Fedora* at the Lirico, and his success this time even surpassed that of the previous season. Rumours had spread through the opera circles of Milan that the tenor had lost his voice during his stay in Russia, but these rumours were soon scotched, and at the end of his season, he confidently boarded the SS *Regina Margherita* on his way to Argentina for his first trip overseas. His South American début in Buenos Aires on the night of 14 May 1899 — again in *Fedora* — was equally successful. Before long, the hitherto unknown tenor was the toast of the Argentinian capital. In the course of a three-month season, he sang in eight different operas, and, as he left Buenos Aires, there was no longer any doubt of his international appeal.

Further challenges — a début in Rome and his first appearances at La Scala in Milan and at the San Carlo in Naples — awaited him upon his return in Italy. He was a much sought-after artist. Offers poured in; his participation in a performance was already beginning to mean a large audience, for opera lovers all over the world clamoured to hear the phenomenal new tenor.

In Naples, where he visited briefly his family and friends, he was greeted as a hero. Old friends, who had once shunned him, fearing he might ask for a loan,

CARUSO'S OWN INTER-PRETATION of himself as Mario Cavaradossi, the hero of Puccini's Tosca. *To his profound disappointment, the tenor was not selected by the composer to create this role at the opera's première in Rome.*

offered him money — now that he didn't need it. Even his sceptical father rejoiced in his new-found success. In Milan, his greeting was even warmer. Suddenly everyone wanted to know Caruso, to be seen with Caruso, to be counted among his friends. No longer worried about money, he was able to live luxuriously. He was generous in his gifts to Ada and to their child, he dined in the best restaurants, was seen at the best cafés, and became known for the elegance and stylishness of his clothing. The portly Neapolitan — he had steadily put on weight — with a working-class background and little education was adjusting with surprising ease to his new position.

Much as he enjoyed his celebrity, there was little time to bask in it. As always, work was more important, and Caruso was soon forced to leave for Rome to prepare for his introductory performances in the Italian capital. Once there, he was faced with the first major disappointment of his professional career. His friendship with Puccini and his personal success in *La Bohème*, had led him to expect a role in the much-heralded world première of Puccini's

ALTHOUGH HE WAS KNOWN for his ability to get along with his colleagues, Caruso made no secret of his contempt for Alessandro Bonci, shown here in the role of Rodolfo in La Bohème. *Caruso's hostility towards Bonci, though somewhat exaggerated by the press, could only have increased when Bonci told an interviewer that he had looked the other way while sitting opposite a pretty woman in a subway, for fear the police would do to him what they had done to Caruso. (He was referring, of course, to the notorious Monkey House Case.)*

new opera, *Tosca*. But it was not to be; that honour would go — for unclear political reasons — to another. Caruso was, understandably, dejected, and in later years he noted that his rejection by Puccini at the time was evidence that 'one's career is neither so brilliant nor so easy as may seem to the casual eyes of the public.'

His career, in fact, had not suffered. Though not selected to sing in the new Puccini opera, Caruso dazzled and thrilled Roman audiences at his début in Mascagni's *Iris* and in two other roles, and his first season in the capital was an overwhelming success. The same can be said of subsequent visits to Russia and Argentina during 1900, where he was once again a favourite with audiences far from home.

Back in Italy, Caruso awaited his most important début to date — at Milan's La Scala in December 1900. Before then, he was finally given the chance to sing the role of Mario Cavaradossi in *Tosca*, first in Treviso and then in Bologna. Bologna was as well known for the severe judgements of its demanding audiences as it was for the high standard of operatic performances given in its Teatro Comunale. Always a difficult and often cruel test for any singer, Bologna presented a special challenge for the young Caruso, for he would be competing with two of Italy's leading tenors, scheduled to sing there during

CARUSO, prominent among those shown in this photograph taken in Montecatini, the well-known Tuscan spa, on 27 September 1900. The tenor had recently returned from a very successful four-month tour of South America.

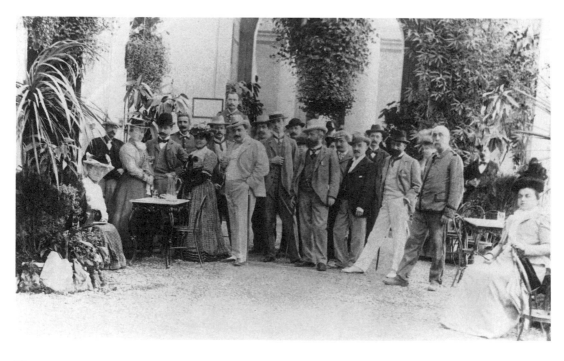

the same season. One of them, Giuseppe Borgatti, had already distinguished himself at La Scala, singing Wagner and creating the title role of Andrea Chénier in Giordano's opera. The other, Alessandro Bonci, had gained considerable popularity for the sweetness of his voice and the refinement of his singing. Both singers, though only a few years older than Caruso, were better known to Bologna's public and seemed to have the advantage over him in what was widely publicized in the press as a battle of the tenors.

Both the press and the public thoroughly enjoyed the combat. Although there were no losers (all three men sang superbly), the one who most favourably impressed the critics was Caruso, who profoundly moved the audience with his interpretation of Puccini's hero on the night of 17 November 1900. It was a gala performance; Giachetti sang the title role, with Eugenio Giraldoni re-creating his original role of Scarpia, and Mugnone conducting, as he had at the opera's première. Puccini, who had supervised rehearsals, wrote to his publisher Giulio Ricordi that the tenor had been 'divine', and following the last of twelve performances he declared that he had never heard a finer interpretation. Ever the cautious diplomat, however, Puccini failed to say what he most probably believed: that he had been wrong to pass over the Neapolitan tenor when choosing the cast for *Tosca*'s première.

THE TEATRO COLÓN, in Buenos Aires, is South America's most important opera house. Caruso made one of his very few appearances with Titta Ruffo in this theatre on 4 August 1915.

5
LA SCALA
and
SAN CARLO

S ince its opening on 3 August 1778, Milan's La
Scala has reigned supreme among the great lyric
theatres of the world. Its exterior is modest, but
its interior, with its horseshoe-shaped auditorium holding
some 3,500 people, is magnificent. Its acoustics are said to
be perfect.

Every great Italian composer — Rossini, Donizetti,
Verdi, Bellini and Puccini — has written one or more
masterpieces for the legendary theatre, and few singers
of note have achieved fame without the approval of La
Scala's discriminating public. To sing at La Scala has been
the goal of singers from all over the world.

Caruso was no exception, but his début there in December 1900, a few weeks after his success in Bologna, was
not an auspicious one. Everything seemed to go wrong,
in spite of widespread predictions of yet another triumph.
During rehearsals of *La Bohème*, the opera which was
to serve as his introduction to the La Scala public, he
clashed with the company's brilliant but strong-willed
thirty-three-year-old musical director, Arturo Toscanini,
already notorious for the extraordinary demands he made
on his singers. The conductor insisted on full voice, even
at early rehearsals, while Caruso preferred to save his full
voice for later. No excuses were accepted at any time, and,
during the rehearsal, though the tenor had pleaded that he
had just eaten and was thus unable to use his full voice, the
enraged conductor put down his baton and only resumed
the rehearsal at the urging of the president of La Scala's
board of directors. As a result, the rehearsal — before a

large audience — did not come to an end until one o'clock in the morning.

Caruso was distraught, and, during the restless night that followed, he became ill, his weary body wracked with fever. Though in a state of panic, he managed to hide his despair, as well as his illness, from the management of La Scala, certain that he would recover in time for his first performance. He had, however, fewer days than he had anticipated. On the morning of 26 December, he was informed that the tenor who was to open the season that night in *Tristan and Isolde* had been taken ill, and that the theatre's management had decided to move *La Bohème* up one night to replace Wagner's opera.

Though this meant that there was even less time than he had hoped in which to recover his strength, Caruso realized that it was impossible for him to turn away from this unique opportunity to sing at a La Scala opening. It was the dream of every singer, and he felt that he might somehow, by a miracle, rise to the occasion.

Nonetheless, his début was, as he had feared, a complete failure. To the astonishment of the elegant audience and to the horror of his colleagues who knew nothing of his illness, Caruso sang badly. Each aria and each act was greeted with silence. Among those most disappointed was Puccini, who had come to the performance eager to witness the triumph of the tenor whose performances in *La Bohème* and *Tosca* had so pleased him, but who left before the final act, too upset to stay until the end.

The following day the critics were devastating in their appraisals of the tenor. According to one, 'The public expected extraordinary surprises from his golden throat and was left baffled; mortified at having been rewarded so poorly for its hopes.' Another questioned whether the role of Rodolfo was simply not suited to Caruso, while one of Caruso's earliest supporters who had enthusiastically praised his performances at the Lirico wondered whether the acoustics were to blame or whether poor health was the cause of his dismal performance.

In spite of this bitter disappointment, Caruso recovered. Again in good health, he proved in the nine further performances of Puccini's masterpiece that his début had simply been an off night for the tenor, and that he was in every way worthy of singing at La Scala. But his real triumph came on the night of 17 February 1901, with his superb singing in Donizetti's *L'Elisir d'Amore*. This time, even

ARTURO TOSCANINI, seen here in a caricature drawn by Caruso, conducted many of the tenor's greatest performances. The two men never became close friends, but each respected the other's artistry.

the harshly critical Toscanini, who conducted the opera, was won over. At the end of the evening, he warmly embraced the tenor and, in a burst of enthusiasm, predicted to Giulio Gatti-Casazza, La Scala's dynamic young managing director, 'By God, if this young Neapolitan continues to sing like this, he will make the whole world talk about him.'

Any reservations on the part of Milan's critics about La Scala's new tenor also disappeared, and they all praised the tenor for the sweetness, the grace and the incomparable facility of his voice. He was, in the words of one, 'a champion, by now rare and precious, of the Italian school of singing which we have taught the whole world'.

GIULIO GATTI-CASAZZA became the managing director of La Scala in 1898, when he was not yet thirty years old. From 1908 to 1935, he performed the same function at the Metropolitan, staging 5,000 performances of 177 works. During that time he became Caruso's valued colleague and friend.

The exhausting Scala season successfully concluded, Caruso embarked once again for South America, with a company led this time by Toscanini. He had had little time to rest, but he had already learned that he could allow himself only short periods of relaxation if he wanted to maintain his position in the competitive world of opera.

He opened the new season in Buenos Aires on 19 May, with a performance of *Tosca*. The conductor was Toscanini, and the evening was a rousing success, with Caruso, greeted like a returning hero, forced to repeat his third-act aria over the angry objections of the fiery maestro, who, then as always, believed that an encore violated the integrity of a composer's score. When, three months later, the season came to a close, Caruso had sung many of his familiar roles and had also appeared for the first and only time in a Wagnerian opera, *Lohengrin*, which he sang three times in Italian. Apparently, it was not a great success, for he never repeated the experience. A few years later, he spoke of this to Adelaide Louise Samson of the *Morning Telegraph* in New York. While he claimed that he hoped to sing again in Wagnerian operas — at least those three works which he considered 'Italian', *Lohengrin, Tristan and Isolde*, and *Die Meistersinger* — he expressed his reservations:

> Wagner did not write his musical dramas for the voice, but for the orchestra. The latter is all important, the voice is merely considered as an instrument ... I personally should fear the effect of a season of Wagner; not only the strain of vocalization, but the strain of the German language on my vocal chords.

At the end of the summer, he returned to Italy, ready for what he was certain would be the most emotionally satisfying engagement of his career to date: his début at the Teatro San Carlo, the most distinguished theatre of his native city of Naples. As a youth, he had often stood before the stately theatre, wondering if he would ever have a chance to sing there. Now, at last, he would have that chance.

He had no doubts that he would triumph there as he had elsewhere. Since he had left Naples, he had inevitably changed. His trim figure had expanded; he had learned to eat and drink well, but had never found the time or the desire to exercise. Through performing in some of the world's great opera houses, he had gained self-confidence: it was reflected in his bearing, the importance he attached to his image, and in the care he took in the selection of his clothes. Most important, he knew he was a far more polished artist than the tenor with a limited range who had left Naples only a few years before.

CARUSO AS NEMORINO, clowning with the great German soprano, Frieda Hempel, in Donizetti's comic opera, L'Elisir d'Amore. *While singing this role on 11 December 1920 Caruso became ill.*

In buoyant, optimistic spirits, Caruso had every reason to expect a warm welcome from his fellow Neapolitans, but his self-confidence and his joy at the very idea of singing at San Carlo had blinded him to the facts of operatic life at the great theatre. More than an opera house, it was, in the words of Daspuro, who was present at Caruso's début there, 'a stormy sea, and the artists, even the most famous, when they came to it were in need of a good pilot and a good knowledge of the public so as not to run up against the rocks and not get stranded on some stage by a sudden change of wind'.

As a Neapolitan who had never lost touch with his native city, Caruso should have understood the complex problems that would face him — or, at least, he should have had a pilot to guide him. He would have to compete with the remembered triumphs of some of the world's greatest tenors who had sung at San Carlo and whose performances had become legendary; and, even worse, he would have to prove himself before one of the most demanding and corrupt audiences in the world, controlled by a powerful, opinionated group of men who believed themselves to be the custodians of the sacred traditions of San Carlo. This extraordinary tribunal of opera-lovers was known as the *sicofanti* (the sycophants). Their subtle signals to their obedient followers in the audience made it clear how each artist should be received.

Surprisingly, Caruso seemed unaware that these *sico-fanti* had to be bought — if not by money, by flattery and the deference they felt due to them from each new artist privileged to sing on the stage of San Carlo. Intoxicated by his past successes away from home, and certain that he would be greeted with open arms by his fellow Neapolitans, Caruso failed to pay proper respect to this tribunal of influential men: he gave out no free tickets, a very common practice, and he made no effort to befriend them or the newspaper critics they controlled. He paid dearly for this.

His San Carlo début, on the night of 30 December 1901, in *L'Elisir d'Amore*, was far from the celebration he had expected. His relatives and old friends welcomed him warmly, but the *sicofanti* were, predictably, cool. During the intermission, they voiced their opinion that the tenor had a competent voice, but that he could certainly not be compared to the great tenors of the past.

The following day, the press echoed the sentiments of the *sicofanti*: Caruso's voice was neither light enough nor sweet enough for Donizetti's comic masterpiece. One critic, Baron Saverio Procida, was particularly severe in his judgement. He not only faulted Caruso's voice — it was, he felt, 'not beautiful' as well as 'baritonal and throaty' — he also felt the tenor's acting had been unconvincing.

Caruso was profoundly hurt by this reception; he had desperately wanted to emerge triumphant before his friends and family. Disappointed and bitter, he cut out Procida's stinging review and carried it with him so that he would never forget his humiliation.

Caruso sang four more performances of Donizetti's opera as well as five performances of Massenet's *Manon*. Following the first performance in *Manon*, he was recognized for his true worth by the public, and, finally, even by the *sicofanti*. Nonetheless, he was never able to forgive the San Carlo public for spoiling what he had hoped and expected would be a memorably happy night. At his later performances, he sang with technical brilliance, but he refused to give all of himself, to share that unique warmth which set him apart from other singers of his time. His performances were good, solid, and professional — no more than that. He gave Neapolitan audiences his voice and his mind, but not his soul.

THE TEATRO SAN CARLO in Naples, where Caruso sang for the first time on the night of 30 December 1901. Bitterly disappointed at the less than enthusiastic reception he received from his fellow Neapolitans on that special night, he vowed never to sing in Naples again — and he kept his promise.

When on 21 January, he sang *Manon* for the last time, Caruso bitterly told Daspuro that Naples would never again hear him sing. 'I will come back to Naples only to see my dear stepmother and eat spaghetti with clams,' he said. And he kept his word.

6

A TRIUMPH
at COVENT
GARDEN

Caruso could afford to turn his back on San Carlo in anger. Though he had not been properly treated in the city of his birth, he had ample proof that he was appreciated and sought after elsewhere. He was negotiating with New York's Metropolitan Opera, a Covent Garden début was in the offing, and, before these, he was to sing in Monte Carlo and at La Scala.

The Monte Carlo season was a short and enormously successful one — Caruso sang in *La Bohème*, and *Rigoletto*. The Milan season consisted solely of fourteen performances of a new and not very well received opera by Alberto Franchetti, *Germania*. But the tenor's short stay in Milan was most important, not because of his season at La Scala, but because it led to his meeting with Fred Gaisberg, the manager of London's Gramophone and Typewriter Company, and a pioneer in the new medium of sound recording. Gaisberg had been sent to Milan in search of artists for a series of records the English company had planned to press, and, upon arrival, had been told that two tenors were causing a sensation at La Scala, and that one or both should be signed up immediately. Gaisberg could hear only one of them — Caruso — and, overwhelmed by the brilliance of the tenor's voice, approached him after a performance of the Franchetti opera to learn what his fee would be. Caruso was intrigued by the offer, and an agreement was quickly concluded. He would sing ten arias for £100, but, because of his busy schedule, all ten selections would have to be recorded in the course of one afternoon.

Gaisberg enthusiastically transmitted these terms to his London office. The reply, cabled at once, was: 'Fee exorbitant, forbid you to record.' Gaisberg, wisely, paid no attention. Instead, he arranged for the recording session, to be held on 11 April 1902 in his suite at the Grand Hotel di Milano. It was an historic occasion, the début of a great recording artist and the birth of a great new industry. Gaisberg recalled the occasion in his memoirs with admirable simplicity: 'One sunny afternoon, Caruso, debonair and fresh, sauntered into our studio and in exactly two hours sang ten arias to the piano accompaniment of Maestro Cottone . . . Not one *stecca*, blemish, or huskiness marred this feat.'

The release of these historic recordings, which were an immediate success, was timed to coincide with Caruso's first appearance at London's Covent Garden, on the night of 14 October, 1902. The opera was one of Caruso's favourites, *Rigoletto*, and singing with him was the great Australian soprano, Nellie Melba. It was a highly significant occasion for two reasons. Firstly, it was the start of an extraordinary relationship between the tenor and the English-speaking audience for whom he became and remained the quintessential Italian tenor — jovial, well fed, with a rich, full sensuous voice, somehow the embodiment of the sunshine of his native land. Secondly, it was the first appearance at Covent Garden of what was to become a legendary partnership between two of the greatest singers of all time.

Caruso and Melba had sung together before — for the first time — the previous February, in *La Bohème*, at the jewel-like opera house in Monte Carlo. It had been a gala performance and a hugely successful one. The soprano, rarely given to excessive praise, remembered the evening in her memoirs.

Caruso absolutely captivated Monte Carlo. As a voice — pure and simple — his was the most wonderful tenor I have ever heard. It rolled out like an organ. It had a magnificent ease, and a truly golden richness.

These were, indeed, rare words of praise from the undisputed queen of opera from Australia ('I put Australia on the map,' she liked to say), who ruled as *prima donna assoluta* wherever she sang.

At that first performance, they made a curious pair: the elegant, ladylike daughter of a prosperous building contractor and the rather awkward, stocky Neapolitan, twelve years her junior. Yet, even in the beginning, Caruso felt sufficiently at ease with the formidable Melba to begin playing those onstage jokes that so often delighted and equally often irritated his colleagues. Melba wrote of one performance of *La Bohème*:

Never shall I forget one night at Monte Carlo . . . how I was suddenly startled in the middle of the death scene by a strange squeaking noise which seemed to come from Caruso as he bent over me. I went on singing but I could not help wondering at the time if Caruso was ill, for his face was drawn and solemn, and every time he bent down there was this same extraordinary noise of squeaking. And then with a gulp which almost made me forget my part, I realized that he had a little rubber toy in his hand, which at the most pathetic phrases he was pressing in my ear.

There were no pranks, however, during the performance of *Rigoletto* on the night Caruso and Melba sang together

THE PROGRAMME *for Caruso's Covent Garden début in* Rigoletto *on 14 May 1902. According to the critic for the* Sunday Times, *the tenor 'proved to be the most gifted vocalist that Italy has sent us for some years past'. It was the beginning of his love affair with the English-speaking public.*

CARUSO

for the first time at Covent Garden. Nor did the relatively inexperienced tenor show any signs of being intimidated either by the presence in the audience of Queen Alexandra or by the existence on stage of the great soprano who ruled as absolute monarch of Covent Garden, where no one dared to cross or challenge her. (Caruso had to be content with a top fee of £399 since Melba alone was permitted to earn as much as £400). His first performance was enthusiastically acclaimed and the following day the critics cheered. 'Signor Caruso' the *Illustrated London News* reported, 'has a vitality and exuberance of expression that carries the audience with him, and a voice that, though powerful, is always melodious.' He was, according to the *Sunday Times*, 'The most gifted vocalist that Italy has sent us for some years past'.

Ten days later, the London public was given its chance to hear Caruso and Melba together in *La Bohème*. It was a performance that confirmed the tenor's popularity and confirmed, too, the magic of his partnership with Melba. 'In the third act of Bohème,' the soprano commented, 'I always feel as if our two voices had merged into one.' (She was not quite so enthusiastic when, at a later performance, the mischievous tenor placed a hot sausage in her hand during the aria, *Che gelida manina*, causing her to hurl the sausage in the air.)

The rest of Caruso's first season at Covent Garden was an unbroken string of dazzling achievements. He sang the role of Edgardo in *Lucia di Lammermoor* so well that the audience remained in their seats to hear the final scene (dominated by the tenor) instead of abandoning the theatre as they usually did after Lucia's spectacular mad scene. He also sang superbly in *Aida, L'Elisir d'Amore, Cavalleria Rusticana*, and, with Melba, in *La Traviata*. He sang too a role he sang only in London, that of Don Ottavio in Mozart's *Don Giovanni*, and, from all reports, he did so magnificently. He was, according to the Russian-born soprano, Felia Litvinne, who sang the role of Donna Anna, 'an incomparable Don Ottavio, with a luminous voice'. She noted further that Caruso was unable to refrain from playing jokes, even during a Mozart opera. 'When he came on the stage, with Donna Anna and Donna Elvira on his arms, for the trio of the masks, he made me laugh by saying, "I am a samovar."'

His triumphant season came to an end on the night of 28 July when he was again paired with Melba in

ANTONIO SCOTTI, Francesco Paolo Tosti, and Caruso in London. Scotti, who had been a favourite at Covent Garden since 1899, urged the management of the London opera house to hire Caruso, and Tosti, an Italian composer of immensely popular songs, who had been appointed singing master to the British royal family, befriended the Neapolitan tenor and introduced him to the 'right' people.

Rigoletto, before one of the most brilliant audiences of the year. London had taken him to its heart. Melba nights had been the highlights of each Covent Garden season since the soprano had started singing there in 1888. Now Caruso nights, too, would be sold out and equally festive and distinguished occasions.

Caruso loved it all. He was growing accustomed to meeting royalty, to contact with the upper strata of society, and he took special delight in his acceptance by the London public in view of what he still remembered bitterly as his rejection by his own people in Naples. On the stage, he enchanted audiences with his impassioned, resonant voice and his memorable interpretations of roles which had not been sung so splendidly in London for many years. Away from the theatre, thanks in large part to his friendships with Paolo Tosti, the Italian composer of popular songs, and Antonio Scotti, the distinguished baritone, he became part of London's musical world. Tosti, who had lived in London for years and was singing teacher to the royal family, was a favourite of English society. He invited Caruso to his Tuesday luncheons at his home near Oxford Street and there introduced him to the right people. Scotti, a fellow Neapolitan who

had first met the tenor in 1899, had been instrumental in arranging for Caruso's Covent Garden début. Seven years older, and considerably more polished and worldly than his colleague (they sang together for the first time that season at Covent Garden), Scotti helped to transform Caruso into a 'gentleman', both in manners and in appearance. In time, the tenor, Tosti and Scotti would preside over a long table at Pagani's, a small restaurant in Great Portland Street behind Queen's Hall, a favourite meeting place of musicians from all over the world — among them, Richard Strauss, Tchaikovsky, Mascagni, Puccini, and Fritz Kreisler — whenever they visited the English capital.

During his first visit to London Caruso also made the acquaintance of the wealthy and beautiful Sybil Seligman, Puccini's closest confidante, who was hostess to every visiting Italian of note and whose elegant home on Upper Grosvenor Street became an unofficial salon during the opera season. There, as elsewhere in London, the Neapolitan tenor became a special favourite, loved for his jovial and warm personality as well as his generosity — he often performed for guests at the Seligman home — and respected for his extraordinary talent.

A jubilant Caruso returned to his home and family in Milan in August 1902. He had reached the top of his profession, but in doing so he had neglected both Ada and their young son. He was deeply attached to both, but he knew his career would always come first and would deny him — as it inevitably denied most performing artists — many of the pleasures of family life. Since his first commitment was not until November, when he was to create the tenor role in Cilea's new opera, *Adriana Lecouvreur*, at Milan's Teatro Lirico, he did have some time to enjoy his family. However, after six highly praised performances in the new opera, he resumed his travels, which over the next few months took him to Trieste, Rome, Lisbon and, once again, to South America — this time, he would make his début in Rio de Janeiro. Before this last trip, he managed to find time to buy his first home, the sumptuous Villa alle Panche in the Tuscan countryside near Florence. It was a significant step for the tenor. Far more than the mere purchase of a house, it represented the fulfilment of a dream, a concrete symbol of his final separation from the crowded, poverty-stricken streets of Naples.

CARUSO MADE HIS triumphant *début in London in 1902, the year this photograph was taken. He was a star, and his bearing, his elegant clothes, and even the turn of his moustache proclaimed it to the world.*

CARUSO

7

FIRST SEASON
at the
METROPOLITAN

Caruso had come a long way from Naples. He had gained fame throughout much of Europe and South America; now it was time to win over the hearts of the North American public, by singing at New York's wealthy and prestigious Metropolitan Opera House.

The Metropolitan had desperately needed a tenor to replace Jean de Reszke, the charming and elegant Pole who had reigned as the company's 'Italian' tenor throughout the last decade of the nineteenth century. De Reszke, whose good manners, impeccable musicianship, and splendid voice had made him a favourite among the members of New York society who patronized the opera house, was at the end of his career — his last performance had taken place at the end of the 1900–01 season, after which, the opera company, though rich in sopranos, was left without a tenor of international stature to sing the Italian repertory.

Caruso was, obviously, just such a singer, but it was not until late in 1903 that he finally came to New York, his arrival there delayed by extended negotiations over contracts, and a change of management at the opera house. Curiously, though de Reszke himself, who had heard Caruso sing in London, had predicted that he would one day be his successor, and though the American press had reported his astounding successes in Europe, no more than the ordinary amount of fanfare surrounded the tenor's first visit to New York.

THE OLD METROPOLITAN OPERA HOUSE on Broadway, between 39th and 40th Streets in New York, was the centre of Caruso's operatic activities from his début in 1903 until his final performance there in 1920. It was replaced in 1966 by a new Metropolitan Opera House, at another location, which lacks the grandeur of the old house.

Accompanied by Ada, he arrived on 11 November 1903, only twelve days before his scheduled début at the opera house. Before that début, there was the inevitable round of interviews with various members of the press. 'He is a wholesome, good-looking person, this young Neapolitan,' one reporter informed his readers. 'He looks as if he ate and fully digested three square meals a day, besides a snack at bedtime.' In spite of this and similar comments concerning his waistline — de Reszke was a strikingly handsome man with a trim figure — Caruso favourably impressed journalists at a press conference held on the afternoon of his arrival. Through an interpreter — he knew little English — he regaled the journalists with humorous stories of his early trials and tribulations and, after playing one of his recordings, advised them that his voice on stage was 'not as worn as it sounded on the machine'. Though these reporters enjoyed making fun of his stoutness and lack of 'refinement', they were charmed by his warmth and boyish exuberance.

That day, too, was Caruso's first chance to meet the man responsible for his coming to New York — Heinrich Conried, the company's Viennese-born managing director. The two men had little in common, least of all language (they used an interpreter), yet a close bond, built on mutual respect, was quickly formed between the stern, iron-fisted manager and the new tenor. Caruso praised the interior of the opera house, its stage, and its technical equipment, which Conried showed him, and the manager was impressed by the tenor's apparent willingness to adhere to the discipline which prevailed at the Metropolitan.

Caruso's début, in *Rigoletto*, on 23 November 1903, the opening night of the season, was also the company's first performance under Conried's direction — the new managing director's experience had previously been in the theatre. Always an occasion for elegance — it was a highlight of the New York social season — this first night was even more festive than usual, for the theatre itself had been extensively and lavishly redecorated. Only the glamorous audience remained unchanged, an audience notoriously more interested in fashion and jewels than in whatever might be happening on stage.

Caruso always maintained that he felt very nervous every time he appeared on stage — it was even an essential prelude to a good performance — but he felt

HEINRICH CONRIED, a Viennese-born actor and manager, was named managing director of the Metropolitan in spite of his lack of experience in the world of opera. He brought Caruso to the New York company in his first year, 1903, and reportedly said that the only performances he enjoyed were those sung by his star tenor.

especially tense as he faced his début at the Metropolitan. He was tired and not yet used to New York, or its pace. His first days in the city had been exhausting ones, with long hours of rehearsals, followed by meetings with strange people in unfamiliar surroundings. He felt very far from home, and he was burdened by what he sensed to be the extraordinary importance for his future of this American début.

Nonetheless, as he left his dressing room and the objects which he had accumulated and served as good luck charms — a rag doll, the figure of a Zulu warrior, a number of pictures of the Madonna — he felt certain that the New York audience would accord him the enthusiastic welcome to which he had become accustomed in Europe and South America. Instead, only a scattering of applause greeted his entrance on stage as the lecherous duke. Somewhat taken aback by the public's indifference — he was apparently unaware that the glamour of the occasion would overshadow the début of any singer — his nervousness increased. Throughout the entire first act, the elegant public reserved whatever enthusiasm it could muster for one person only, the immensely popular, brilliant Polish soprano, Marcella Sembrich.

However, the difficult-to-please audience warmed to the new tenor in the second act, and his interpretation of the unfailingly popular *La Donna é Mobile* roused the public to call for an encore in the third, but at no point during the entire performance did Caruso receive anything that might be called an overwhelming ovation. Nevertheless, though far from the memorable triumph that might have been expected, Caruso's début was far from a failure. He sang well, but he had the misfortune of singing before a public that cared little about the art of singing — at least at the opening performance.

Critics the following day were, for the most part, more appreciative and enthusiastic than the audience had been. Though not unanimous or lavish in their praise, they generally agreed that the opera company had acquired a first-rate tenor. The tenor himself, in public at least, expressed satisfaction, politely informing a reporter that he was delighted with his reception:

> It was superb, splendid. I had no idea that such a thing could be in America . . . Such an appreciation of wonderful music, such an appreciation of myself — far beyond my wildest dreams . . . New York has opened its arms to me, a stranger, and I embrace it.

Though not a completely accurate account of what had happened at the Metropolitan opening that night — for New York had not yet opened its arms to him nor had he yet embraced the city — it was soon obvious that the first season at the Metropolitan was the beginning of an enduring love affair between the Neapolitan tenor and the American public. But the love affair began rather cautiously and its beginning was somewhat delayed. The nervous strain which had preceded his first performance, together with New York's harsh climate, took its toll following that first performance, and Caruso's next two scheduled appearances, in *La Bohème* and *Rigoletto*, had to be cancelled because of an attack of tonsillitis. By the time he was ready to sing, in *Aida* on 30 November, it was clear that he was still not in full possession of his vocal powers — at least in the first two acts.

His singing of *Celeste Aida* at the beginning of the opera was tentative, and until the third act he showed uncharacteristic restraint. But with the dramatic Nile scene of the third act, he finally unleashed the full force

MARCELLA SEMBRICH, a brilliant Polish soprano, born in 1858, was a great favourite at the Metropolitan. She sang the role of Gilda in Rigoletto *at Caruso's New York début.*

of his voice. From then on, his triumph was a resounding one. The Metropolitan audience, above all, those who filled the upper balconies of the opera house, showed signs, for the first time, of the tremendous affection it would bestow on the tenor for the rest of his life.

A few nights later, Caruso sang in *Tosca*, confirming his growing popularity with the public. New York critics, too, praised his vocal skills, though they were almost unanimous in faulting his dramatic interpretation for lacking what one called 'aristocratic flavour', or 'distinction of bearing'. There was a certain condescension in some of the criticism; Caruso was not the distinguished figure de Reszke had been. The reviewer for the *Press* wrote:

He indulged frequently in the *voix blanche*, dear to the Italians but disagreeable to the Americans. He achieved some fine climaxes, however, especially in the early part of the third act, and so worked upon the feelings of the Italian contingent in his audience that he was forced to repeat a whole passage, greatly to the detriment of the dramatic integrity of the scene. The applause continued even after his concession to popular feeling . . .

Only a reporter for the *Telegraph* pointed out the true significance of the tenor's first *Tosca*:

> Caruso leapt into the hearts of the audience. Henceforth he will probably be as popular as idols of years gone by. Caruso sang for the third time in this country last night, and only last night he arrived.

For most reviewers, however, Caruso did not really arrive until the afternoon of 5 December, when he sang for the first time in *La Bohème*, with Marcella Sembrich. The critics were unanimous. 'Mr Caruso showed yesterday afternoon for the first time since he has been in this country the supreme beauty of his voice . . . such a one as has not been enjoyed here for a long time,' wrote the critic for the *Times*. The reviewer for the *Herald* considered the tenor's singing so exciting that even Sembrich responded, singing her role as never before. The reviewer wrote:

> Mr Caruso outdid himself, and fairly inspired his fellow artist . . . Mme Sembrich's recognition of his great singing was gracefully shown when at the curtain call she impulsively plucked a blossom from her bouquet and pressed it into his hand.

It was the beginning of another brilliant partnership; his colleagues enjoyed singing with Caruso and they sang their best when performing with him. Over the next few weeks, Caruso and Sembrich sang together in *Pagliacci*, *La Traviata* and *Lucia di Lammermoor*, but their greatest success came in the new production of *L'Elisir d'Amore*. As had happened at La Scala, Caruso's singing made the work one of the most popular of the entire repertory. The critics this time were as ecstatic as were the audiences. It was, in the words of one reviewer, 'a splendid success'.

Caruso began to show signs of fatigue towards the end of his first visit to New York — a short one, since he had to honour commitments previously made in Europe — and he seemed especially tired at his last performance in *L'Elisir d'Amore* on the night of 8 February, when in the midst of a duet with Sembrich, his voice faltered. But the public, for whom he could by now do no wrong, seemed unconcerned, and the tenor quickly recovered, singing his last-act aria with his customary brilliance. In spite of his protests he was forced to repeat the aria.

Caruso, in a remarkably short time, had established a unique, almost intimate rapport with the New York public. What he lacked in elegance and style he made up by the sheer force and beauty of his voice and the magnetic warmth of his personality. De Reszke had been greatly admired, but he had kept himself at a distance from his public. The Neapolitan, with his simple charm and ready wit, was a popular tenor, in the true meaning of the word, one with whom the people — many of them recent Italian immigrants, who filled the upper balconies of the opera house — could identify.

JOHN McCORMACK and Jean de Reszke. McCormack and Caruso were never rivals, as sometimes reported; instead they were good friends and each admired the other's talent. De Reszke, an elegant, handsome Polish tenor, born in 1850, combined superb musicianship and a voice of extraordinary beauty. He was the Metropolitan's leading tenor in the pre-Caruso years.

His last performance that season took place on the night of 10 February when the opera was *Lucia di Lammermoor*. When the tenor was about to sail for Europe a few days later, an enormous gathering of his new friends and admirers crowded the pier to say goodbye. Caruso, genuinely moved at the outpouring of affection shown to him, was gracious in his farewell remarks. A reporter quoted him as saying:

> My audiences have been everything to me, and I am very sorry I could not have gone on singing in answer to their desire. Of course, I love my dear America — she is beautiful, generous, and I shall come back to her next year.
>
> The critics — they were kind, except about my fat and my clothes. I shall train down next year and wear better — what you call them? — pantaloons and coats. Then the critics will have nothing to criticize.

8
The KING
of SONG

By 1904, word of Caruso's musical triumphs and of his unique rapport with his audiences had spread, and opera companies all over the world vied for his services. A Caruso appearance was a guarantee of a full and an enthusiastic house.

Before the tenor returned to New York the following November, he gave performances in Monte Carlo, Paris, Barcelona, Prague, Dresden, Berlin, and, twice, in London. These engagements were all, with one exception, immensely successful. The exception was Barcelona, the scene of one of the few complete failures of Caruso's astounding career.

Contemporary accounts of his brief stay in Spain differ in detail, but all agree that Caruso's Spanish début was a disaster, and that the cause was most probably not to be found in the performance itself, but rather in the enormous publicity build-up that preceded that performance. (It was only the first of many times that this would happen to the tenor.) His arrival had been widely heralded, and along with word of his extraordinary talent, there had been reports that he would be receiving the enormous sum of 7,000 pesetas for each of two scheduled performances of *Rigoletto*. This news was greeted with anger and resentment by the proud Spanish public, for their country was the home of the legendary tenor Julián Gayarré, and even he had never made such exorbitant demands. In addition, the high fee paid to Caruso meant that there was little money left to pay other members of

GERALDINE FARRAR, the small, slender, beautiful and exceptionally glamorous American soprano, sang many memorable performances with Caruso. Her best-known roles were Madame Butterfly and Carmen, both of which she sang with Caruso.

CARUSO

the cast with the result that second-rate singers were hired to support the new tenor, as happened all too often during Caruso's career.

The public's resentment meant that the evening was a failure even before it began. At first Caruso was greeted coolly, but before long the audience's indifference turned to open anger. What little applause there was, was countered by hisses, so disruptive that the performance was interrupted several times. Caruso, at first puzzled by the unexpected response, soon became enraged. According to Richard Barthélemy, his long-time accompanist and friend, the tenor became so unnerved during the last act of the opera that he brandished his sword menacingly at those hostile members of the audience, seated at the front of the auditorium, who had noisily interfered with his performance.

When the final curtain fell, there was complete silence. The indignant tenor left Barcelona at once. Just as he had

vowed never again to sing in Naples, he swore now that he would never again sing in Barcelona or, indeed, in any Spanish theatre.

The Barcelona fiasco was an isolated incident, and the tenor's successes far outweighed this one failure. Among these successes during this period, one stood out — his season at Monte Carlo which immediately followed his triumphant first season at the Metropolitan. It was memorable not merely for the brilliance of Caruso's reception — at each appearance he was greeted with delirious applause — but because it was during that season that he first sang with another soprano who would be one of his great partners. The opera was, again, *La Bohème*, and the soprano this time was the American, Geraldine Farrar. Unlike Melba, with whom Caruso had triumphed in the same opera and in the same theatre two years earlier, Farrar was young — she had just celebrated her twenty-second birthday — and she was strikingly beautiful. She was at the beginning of her career; she had made her début in Berlin in 1901 and had not yet sung opera in her own country. Her appearance as Mimi in *La Bohème* marked her Monte Carlo début; it was also her first opportunity to sing with a tenor of Caruso's stature.

She approached her introduction to the celebrated tenor with apprehension, but she was soon put at ease. 'Never shall I forget the apparition that walked into the first rehearsal,' she wrote in her memoirs. She continued:

Clad in shrieking checks, topped by a grey fedora, yellow gloves grasping a gold-headed cane, he jauntily walked on to the stage. A happy smile illumined a jolly face, which was punctuated by the two largest black eyes I have ever seen.

Jean de Reszke, then retired and teaching singing in Nice, was among those present at that first rehearsal, but Caruso — as was his custom — did not sing full voice for him or for anyone else then or at later rehearsals. Because of this, Farrar was astounded when she heard the tenor on the night of the first performance. 'When I heard those rich and glorious tones rise above the orchestra, I was literally stricken dumb with admiration', she remembered. The performance, on the night of 10 March 1904, was a milestone in the fabulously successful soprano's career. Caruso, too, was delighted with the magic that he and the beautiful young American generated together, and he made no secret of it. 'After the third act, and in full view of the audience,' Farrar wrote, 'Caruso lifted me bodily and carried me to my dressing room in the general wave of enthusiasm.'

Not only audiences but other singers — his partners as well as those who heard him perform during these years — were enchanted with Caruso's enormous talent. Frieda Hempel, the marvellously versatile German soprano, then only nineteen years old, was seated in the balcony on the night, in October 1904, when the tenor made his successful début in Berlin.

> When I arrived home in a state of agitation, I attempted to describe my impressions to my parents. 'It is as if I sank into a deep velvet armchair so soft, so tender, so velvety,' I said. 'Caruso's singing was so perfect, so heavenly! It is a true miracle that a man should possess such a God-given voice.'

Anna Eugenie Schoen-Rene, a soprano who became an outstanding singing teacher, attended Caruso's performance in Berlin that year and also had a chance to watch him during rehearsals. She was profoundly impressed, not only with his voice, but also with his behaviour during rehearsals:

> He never wished to be treated as a star, or to set himself apart from other singers. I noticed at the rehearsals that many of the other experienced singers thought it not worth while to go to rehearsals arranged to prepare new soloists; but Caruso was invariably on hand — though he needed extra rehearsals less than any of them — and every newcomer was given his cordial co-operation.

Sopranos and great tenors of the past, like Tamagno and de Reszke, appreciated Caruso the man and the artist. Contemporary tenors, potential rivals, also valued his artistry and friendship. Among these was John McCormack, the Irish tenor who first heard Caruso sing with the San Carlo opera company at Covent Garden in the autumn of 1904 — Caruso had vowed never again to sing in Naples, but had not said that he would refuse to sing with the opera company, and a chance to sing with them

RESTAURANT.

No. of Table.........Covers.......

DINNERS.

Date..........

WHILE DINING AT THE SAVOY in London with his friend John McCormack, Caruso made these two caricatures of the great tenors looking at each other in their wine glasses.

in London seemed a unique opportunity to get back at the Neapolitans who had so rudely rejected him.

It had been an enormously successful season for Caruso (and for Rina Giachetti, Ada's sister, who made her London début then), and McCormack, then only twenty years old, never forgot the Neapolitan's performance in *La Bohème*:

> When I listened to the opening phrases of Puccini's music, sung by that indescribably glorious voice as Caruso alone could sing, my jaw dropped as though hung on a hinge. Such smoothness and purity of tone, and such quality; it was like a stream of liquid gold ... The sound of Caruso's voice that night lingered in my ears for months, and will doubtless linger there always. It will always be to me one of the memorable moments of my life.

Later the two men met frequently but, though often labelled as such, they were never rivals. McCormack was often called the Irish Caruso, but he realized he was no Caruso. His voice, pure and very beautiful, was far lighter and less robust than that of his Italian colleague. Instead, the two singers became good friends, sharing a love of singing and of a good joke. It has been reported that McCormack once asked Caruso, 'How is the world's greatest tenor?' To which Caruso answered, 'Since when have you become a baritone?' 'Rival or no rival,' McCormack said many years later, 'there has never been a man whom I loved so much as Caruso. There has never been one like him, and there will never be another.'

Caruso's eagerly anticipated second visit to the United States was notable not only as his first full season at the Metropolitan, but also as his first introduction to the vast American public that lay beyond New York.

The Metropolitan season was in every way a splendid one, during which the tenor dazzled the New York public by singing a total of twelve roles — nine of them during the first five weeks of that season. It was an astounding achievement. In addition to enriching the opera company musically, Caruso managed to change the character of the austere opera house, in a remarkably short time, drawing to it not only the members of New York society — for opera had been one of the favourite pastimes of the upper classes — but also masses of people who had never before

entered the theatre, infusing the elegant auditorium with a vitality it had never known before. Opera had been a popular entertainment in Italy, but never, until the arrival of Caruso, in America.

Everywhere the tenor went, he made news, and he enjoyed himself and his fame thoroughly. He gave private concerts at the homes of the city's wealthiest families, and he instructed Italian-American chefs in the art of preparing pasta at restaurants wherever he dined. He continued to enjoy on-stage pranks: during a performance of *La Gioconda*, he pressed a raw egg into the hand of a horrified baritone, who did his best to enact the role of the sinister spy Barnaba while wondering what to do with the crushed egg. He also spent long hours in his suite at the Hotel York, carefully studying the nuances of each new role. There was always time for play, but above all it was his work that absorbed Caruso; every detail, dramatic and historic as well as vocal, was an important part of his preparation for each role, as he strove to become a complete artist and not merely a golden-voiced singer.

When the Metropolitan season ended, Caruso set out for his first encounter with the audiences who lived far from New York. Through his recordings (he had made five more records with Victor in February 1905) and through an intensive publicity campaign, (he was already widely known as the King of Song), his fame had spread rapidly from coast to coast; but the majority of Americans had not yet had an opportunity to experience the magic of a Caruso performance.

This first cross-country tour took him to Boston, Pittsburgh, Cincinnati, Chicago, Minneapolis, Omaha, Kansas City, San Francisco and Los Angeles. He was greeted everywhere with thunderous applause, extending his kingdom from one side of the country to the other. When, after the tour, he left for Europe in late April, he was more than satisfied with his long stay in America; pleased, too, that this time there had been far fewer comparisons made to the great de Reszke. And, when those comparisons were made, they often echoed the judgement of the critic James Huneker, probably America's most erudite and knowledgeable critic of the arts, who wrote in the March 1905 issue of *Success Magazine* that one note from Caruso's golden throat was 'worth, in a purely tenoric way, all of Jean's voice'. From then on, all tenors would be compared to only one — Caruso.

After a two-month season at Covent Garden and a few lesser engagements late in the summer, Caruso was finally able to leave for Italy and his first chance to relax in many months. This he did not find easy and never would. His successes had been the result of intensive work. In addition to his performances, which drained much of his energy, he spent much of his time away from the theatre in hotel suites, vocalizing and studying new roles. The short periods between engagements rarely allowed him enough time to unwind.

Because of this, the periods at 'home', in the Tuscan countryside, were especially welcome. Apparently, however, Caruso had not been satisfied with the first of his villas, for, only a year after buying the Villa alle Panche, he bought the even more luxurious Villa Campi, perched on the hills near the village of Lastra a Signa, near Florence.

His first holiday there, a year earlier, had given him a chance to spend time with his young son, Fofò, but it had already become obvious that the demands of his performing schedule would always restrict such periods to a minimum. And, because Giachetti, too, was unable to devote enough time to their child — when not pursuing her own faltering singing career, she accompanied Caruso on his travels — a decision was made to send the five-year-old boy to a boarding school outside Florence in the autumn. It had been a difficult decision, complicated further by the birth of a second son, christened Enrico Jr, but known as Mimmi, on 7 September 1904.

During his second holiday there, in 1905, Caruso again did his best to enjoy his time with his family as well as the fruits of his professional triumphs. His new home, which he had renamed the Villa Bellosguardo, was a splendid house, standing in the midst of a huge park. There were formal gardens, many acres of vineyards, and several lawn tennis courts — something he had learned to appreciate as a status symbol, even though he had not learned to play the game. The 'castle' itself, as Caruso called it, had an illustrious history, having once belonged to Dante's friend, Guido Cavalcanti. Originally built of rough-hewn stone, it had been renovated and modernized to a luxuriously high standard, and Caruso took great pride in showing it off to the members of the press, who visited him during his stay there. There were two floors. On the ground floor were two salons, a chapel, a forty-foot-long drawing room, kitchens, a baggage room, and completely separate servants' quarters. On the upper floor were twenty more rooms, among them a gallery of arms, an art gallery, an Arabian conservatory, a special room for Caruso's growing coin collection (one of his few diversions), and an immense studio.

Although he complained that, because of his work, he was able to spend far too little time in the country with his family, it was obvious that he could not really enjoy either the country or, for very long, the company of his family. He was born in a large, noisy, teeming city, and gardens and vineyards had never interested him — except for the food and wine they might produce. Although he loved and often enjoyed his family, it would always come second to his demanding profession. The imposing Villa Bellosguardo was a potent symbol of his success and not a source of deep satisfaction. Satisfaction came almost exclusively from his work. A holiday in his luxurious home allowed him to spend time with those he loved, but, above all, it granted him a peaceful period in which to study his operatic roles, refreshing the old ones as well as learning the new, and, to a somewhat lesser extent, an interval during which he could catch his breath between his exhausting engagements.

THE MAGNIFICENT VILLA BELLOSGUARDO, near Florence in the heart of Tuscany, was more than a summer home to Caruso: it was a symbol of his unprecedented success.

9

TWO ORDEALS: *An* EARTHQUAKE *and an* ACCUSATION

A chronicle of Caruso's engagements, when the tenor was at the zenith of his vocal powers, would be monotonous. One brilliant performance followed another, wherever he sang — in London, Vienna, Berlin, Hamburg, and, of course, New York — during 1905 and 1906. Thunderous ovations were the rule. As the critic for the New York newspaper, the *Sun*, W.F. Henderson, noted, 'New York is no longer opera-mad, but Caruso-mad . . . The fact now to be recorded is that the public has gone to the opera in the season just ended, almost solely for the purpose of hearing Enrico Caruso.'

Caruso's fame had spread far beyond the confines of the opera house. He was a personality known to those who had never heard an opera, and his every move, off stage as well as on, no matter how insignificant, was reported by the press. His private life — though with his arduous performing schedule there was little time for it — was the subject of close scrutiny. Recognizing the advantages to his career, Caruso willingly granted endless interviews. He did not find these easy — his English was still poor and he usually spoke in halting French — but his magnetic charm rarely failed to delight those journalists who took every opportunity to report details of the off-stage life and habits of the man one reporter called 'Herr Conried's thousand-dollar-an-hour tenor'.

The image of an affable, relaxed family man emerged from these articles. Caruso was, according to the press, happily married and comfortably settled, and the dark-

CARUSO

CARUSO AS DON JOSÉ in
Carmen. *He sang the role on
the night of the earthquake in
San Francisco, and he had
sung it for the first time in
1896 in Salerno. At that first
performance he had failed to
reach the high note at the end
of the 'Flower Song'.*

eyed beautiful Ada, exquisitely dressed in her Parisian gowns, was often at his side as he entertained reporters with stories of his Neapolitan childhood, and as he both created and refuted legends that had become part of his image. He did not, he declared (contradicting a legend he himself created), fill his dressing room with dolls or fetishes; when nervous before a performance, he thought with love of his dead mother. He denied that he owned several hundred waistcoats, but the dapper, neatly moustached tenor (he was seen with and without a moustache at different times in his career) admitted that he paid great attention to what he wore. If the day was dark, he donned bright colours; if it was sunny, he favoured black suits.

Food, he confessed, was important to him, and his own chef accompanied him in his travels through America. Though one journalist wrote that he had 'a spaghetti appetite', the tenor maintained that he ate lightly and regularly, but well. He drank moderately, preferring the wine of his own country, but he smoked incessantly, boasting that cigarettes did not harm him in the least.

He was, without a doubt, the brightest and wealthiest star in the world of opera. The luxury of his New York home on 57th Street and the flourishes with which his valet greeted visitors were evidence of his enormous wealth; yet Caruso's warmth, ready wit, and good nature enabled him, without apparent effort, to project the image of a simple and generous man — the people's tenor.

Americans loved him, and he reciprocated by loving Americans, finding the skyscrapers 'extraordinary', President Theodore Roosevelt 'great', and American women 'fine'. Yet in spite of his string of successes in the United States, it was there, in 1906, that he endured two of the most disturbing experiences of his life, both of them because he was at the wrong place at the wrong time.

The first took place at the end of a Metropolitan cross-country tour that had begun in March 1906. It had started well, in Baltimore, where more than 3,000 spectators crowded into the 2,300-seat Lyric Theatre to hear the tenor sing in *Martha*. During the next stop, in Washington, Caruso was visited in his dressing room by President Theodore Roosevelt, who invited him to the White House and presented him with a large signed photograph. Pittsburgh, Chicago, St Louis, and Kansas City followed, then the company departed for what was to be a two-week season in San Francisco.

TWO ORDEALS: *An* EARTHQUAKE *and an* ACCUSATION

Caruso, uncharacteristically, showed signs of fatigue when he finally arrived in the Golden Gate city. Over a period of twenty-five days, he had sung six different roles in thirteen performances, and was not his usual jovial self when greeted by journalists on arrival in San Francisco. He was not only exhausted from his demanding schedule, but also showed deep concern over reports about the recent eruption of Mount Versuvius, which had resulted in the deaths of more than 2,000 of his fellow countrymen and had destroyed the homes of countless thousands of others.

The entire company seemed worn out by its travels. The season opened with Carl Goldmark's *The Queen of Sheba*, never a very popular opera, which was given a listless performance by its weary cast and was coolly received by the public. The second performance, of *Carmen*, presented the following night, proved far more satisfactory, largely because of Caruso's presence in the cast. Olive Fremstad, singing the title role, was not in good voice, but the evening was more than redeemed by the tenor's superb interpretation of the role of Don José. So thoroughly did he dominate the performance that Blanche Partington, of the *San Francisco Call*, wrote in her review, '*Carmen* rechristened itself for San Francisco last night. For the season, at least, it is *Don José*. Caruso is the magician.'

It was a review that few San Franciscans ever had a chance to read, for early on the morning of 18 April

NOB HILL, SAN FRANCISCO, on 18 April 1906, following the earthquake and fires which devastated the northern Californian city. Caruso had sung in Carmen *a few hours before the disaster struck and never forgot the terrifying experience. 'Give me Vesuvius,' he reportedly told reporters later.*

CARUSO

1906, the great San Andreas fault, which extends the length of the California coast, settled violently, causing an earthquake which, together with the fires that followed, nearly wiped out their city, destroying more than 28,000 buildings, including the opera house which had been the scene of Caruso's triumph.

The first tremor was felt at 5.13 in the morning, while the tenor slept in his elegantly appointed suite at the Palace, the city's most luxurious hotel. He later described his initial reactions to a reporter from the *Sketch* of London:

> I wake up about five o'clock, feeling my bed rocking as though I am in a ship on the ocean, and for the moment I think I am dreaming that I am crossing the water on my way to my beautiful country. And so I take no notice for the moment, and then, as the rocking continues, I get up and go to the window, raise the shade and look out. And what I see makes me tremble with fear. I see the buildings toppling over, big pieces of masonry falling, and from the street below I hear cries and screams of men and women and children.
>
> I remain speechless, thinking I am in some dreadful nightmare, and for something like forty seconds I stand there, while the buildings fall and my room still rocks like a boat on the sea. And then I gather my faculties together and call for my valet. He comes rushing in, quite cool, and, without any tremor in his voice, says: 'It is nothing.' But all the same he advises me to dress quickly and go in the open, lest the hotel fall and crush us to powder.

It was the beginning of a nightmare for Caruso as it was for all those present that night in San Francisco. The ordeal lasted more than twenty-four hours. Accounts of Caruso's behaviour and movements vary, from observer to observer, but he insisted that, though frightened, he never lost his head. Arnold Genthe, a photographer, wrote that he found him at the Hotel St Francis, a few blocks from the Palace, wearing a fur coat over his pyjamas, and muttering, ''Ell of a place. I never come back here.' Another observer heard him trying, in vain, to reach a high C in the corridor of his hotel. His friend Scotti told reporters that he had found Caruso wandering around Union Square, a towel wrapped around his neck to protect his throat, and the framed photograph of President Roosevelt in his hand. According to Scotti, both he and Caruso took refuge in the home of a friend, Dr Arthur Bachman, where they spent the night, with Caruso choosing to sleep under a tree rather than risk having the house fall on him. One thing seems certain: throughout the ordeal, Caruso proudly held on to the signed photograph of the American president, which served as his identification as well as a passport through the barricades erected by the police and army in an attempt to maintain some degree of order amidst the chaos.

On the morning of 19 April, Caruso and the other members of the opera company managed to reach Oakland, across the bay, where they boarded a train for the long journey to New York. Caruso was still shaken when he arrived and reportedly told journalists, 'Give me Vesuvius.' The terrifying experience was not soon forgotten, and Caruso never forgave the city of San Francisco; it joined Naples and Barcelona on the list of cities in which he vowed he would never sing again.

Caruso had survived the devastating earthquake, but, only seven months later, he was to endure a far more painful experience, the most senselessly humiliating ordeal of his life. Following the earthquake, he had returned to Europe for another series of spectacular triumphs; critics agreed that his performances had surpassed their and the public's greatest expectations. Unanimously acclaimed as the greatest tenor of his time, he was, apparently, invincible. But, shortly after his arrival in New York, his emotional strength was to be tested as it had never been tested before.

His ordeal began innocently, with a walk through New York's Central Park zoo and a stop in front of the monkey house, but it resulted in an incident that threatened to destroy the tenor's entire American career. It became known as the 'Monkey House Case', and newspapers throughout the world delighted in reporting, with varying degrees of accuracy, every detail of the trials and agony of the great idol of the operatic world.

The shocking story broke on the morning of 17 November 1906; it was front-page news. Caruso had been arrested the previous afternoon for molesting an innocent woman. Patrolman James J. Kane, who made the arrest and soon enthusiastically assumed the role of the tenor's nemesis, told of observing a well-dressed man standing suspiciously close to a woman in front of one of the monkey cages and of seeing the woman suddenly move away from the man, calling him a loafer and threatening to have him arrested. At this point, Kane stepped in: he arrested the man and led him to a nearby police station.

Once there, Caruso vigorously protested his innocence, but the woman, who identified herself as Hannah Graham, insisted that he had annoyed her as many as three or four times before she threatened him with arrest. She was told to appear at the police court the following morning, and the horrified tenor was led away to another police station where he was arraigned and ordered to be locked up. Confused and near hysteria, unable to understand fully the charges made against him and unable to make himself understood, he was restrained by two policemen and forced into a cell.

Caruso remained there for only a short time. Once he had regained his composure, he asked that a note be sent to Heinrich Conried, asking for the managing director to be brought to the police station. Conried came at once and provided the bail required for the release of the tenor.

Once Caruso returned to his home, he issued a statement, denying all charges and protesting about his treatment at the hands of the police. Conried realized how the press would treat the story of his prize tenor's humiliation and immediately called an informal press conference. There he angrily denounced the arrest as 'ridiculous, absolutely ridiculous'.

The following morning, neither Caruso nor his accuser — no one named Graham lived at the address she had given — turned up at the police court. A certificate was presented which stated that the tenor was unable to leave his home because of a painful attack of sciatica, while Mrs Graham simply did not show up. Nevertheless, the zealous Patrolman Kane declared he would find her by the following Wednesday, the date set for the postponed hearing. The policeman obviously enjoyed his new role as defender of American womanhood and was readily available to any and all journalists, boasting to all who would listen that he was accustomed to making at least twenty arrests a month and that some of those arrested were prominent actors and Wall Street brokers, some of them 'folks worth millions'.

The press, too, was having a field day, reporting each and every development (or non-development) in the scandal, and as the time for the tenor's court appearance drew

n, SATURDAY, NOVEMBER 17, 1906.

Caruso and His Overcoat Pocket as Policeman Kane Describes I

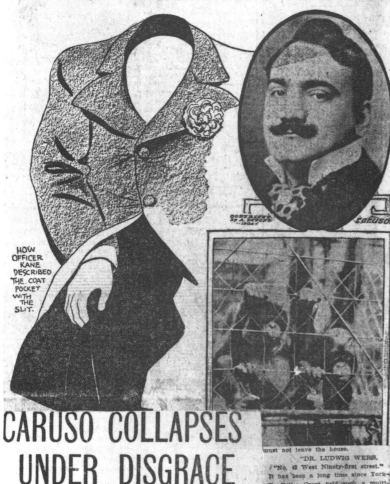

HOW OFFICER KANE DESCRIBED THE COAT POCKET WITH THE SLIT.

must not leave the house.

"DR. LUDWIG WEISS.

"No. 42 West Ninety-first street."

It has been a long time since Yorkville Police Court held such a multitude as the prospect of the arraignment of Caruso attracted. Half an hour before the time for opening court there was a mass-meeting of photographers on the front steps, and so many reporters packed the space inside the courtroom rail that the officers had to form mass plays to get the prisoners to Magistrate Baker's bench. An early but quiet arrival was Justice Truax, of the Supreme Court, who conferred at length with the Magistrate in his private office. It is understood that Justice Truax visited Yorkville Court in Caruso's interest.

CARUSO COLLAPSES UNDER DISGRACE OF ARREST IN ZOO

Sends Physician's Certificate that He Is Too Ill to Appear in Police Court to Answer to the Woman's Charge.

Tenor Broken Down.

Promptly at 9 o'clock a big red automobile rolled up to the court-house and two men alighted. One wore a slig hat, a profusion of hair, a little mustache and a fur-trimmed overcoat. "That's him," shouted the photographers, but it wasn't. The man with the hat and the hair proved to be John Viafora, of No. 24 Manhattan avenue, an artist and a close friend of Caruso. It appears that the tenor was on his way to Mr. Viafora's house yesterday afternoon when he stopped into the dwelling place of the Central Park monkeys and got into trouble with Mrs. Graham.

Sig. Enrico Caruso, the star tenor of the Metropolitan Opera-House, failed to make his advertised debut in Yorkville Police Court to-day. Mrs. Hannah Graham, the young matron who had him arrested yesterday on a charge of annoying her in the monkey-house at Central Park, was another absentee. Lawyers representing Caruso presented a certificate reading as follows:

This is to certify that Mr. Enrico ... tack of sciatica, due to exposure, which prevents him from being absent. He

near, public opinion, as reflected in the press, began to shift towards Caruso. There had been too many wild charges of dubious validity, too many unfounded rumours; and, most important, Mrs Graham was still nowhere to be found.

She was still missing on the afternoon of 21 November when hearings of the case began. Other witnesses were produced by the prosecution, but the testimonies were contradictory. The case against the tenor, seated in the courtroom with Scotti and Conried, was completely unconvincing, in spite of the impassioned attack of Deputy Commissioner Mathot, representing the police, who railed against the crowd of Italian-Americans who filled the courtroom, some of whom he labelled 'curs and perverts'.

This attack and the flimsy evidence against him meant that, when the verdict was announced the following day, a wave of shock swept through the court. Caruso was found guilty and fined ten dollars, the minimum fine permitted for the charge of disorderly conduct. The cries of indignation that followed were understandable. They came not only from Caruso's attorney, who immediately filed an appeal, but even from such an unlikely source as the former Chief of Police, William S. Devery, who told reporters that the arrest was an 'outrage, and his conviction was based on no evidence at all'. Echoing the sentiments of most of those who had followed the case, he was deeply disturbed by the anti-foreigner approach of the prosecution. 'It won't do to abuse foreigners just because they are foreigners,' he stated. 'The police have more to do than to hang around the monkey house and look for victims for purposes that are not on the level.'

Caruso was profoundly disturbed by the totally unexpected verdict, but, outwardly at least, he remained calm, encouraged by the heartfelt messages of support he received from singers and other colleagues (Puccini and Jean de Reszke among them) from all over the world. Most representatives of the international press, which had given the episode extensive coverage, also sided indignantly with the tenor. Many members of the Italian press found the whole affair just one more indication that Americans simply could not understand the sophisticated European mentality. A writer for the influential *Il Tempo* of Milan noted that the Italian ladies 'are eager to be rubbed against by tenors, because, like hunchbacks, they bring good luck'.

A DESPERATE NOTE from Caruso, imploring a friend to come to New York's 67th Street police station following the tenor's arrest at the Monkey House.

On the other hand, some journalists, including some American reporters, treated the matter humorously. New York's *Morning Telegraph* reported that Caruso had had a picture removed from his suite at the Hotel Savoy because it was entitled 'The Monks of St Simian', and had had a bellboy fired for whistling the tune of 'I've Got a Feeling for You'. The *Musical Courier* noted that the betting was one thousand to one that the muff Musetta would hand Mimi in the last act of *La Bohème* would not be made of monkey fur.

Even one of New York's leading Italian-language newspapers — there were several at the time, serving the growing community of Italian immigrants — found the episode amusing, though the target of the newspaper's sarcasm was not Caruso but rather the puritanical American way of life. The article began:

> Enrico Caruso has been condemned to pay a fine of ten dollars. May the Lord be praised! May St Ursula with her thousands of little angels exult in the heights of the heavens! Justice is done. The modesty of the Americans is saved. The great tenor has paid the penalty of his depraved appetite . . .
>
> Caruso is condemned. The police have triumphed. The police, who are blind to the infractions of law, by day and by night, in saloons, hotels, concert halls and the innumerable places that corrupt the young and scandalize all. These honest police may be satisfied, for they have convinced a judge and a puritanical people that they caught Caruso patting a modest American woman, who has not been found.

It was, however, no laughing matter for Caruso or for the management of the Metropolitan Opera House. The tenor had been deeply hurt and embarrassed by the episode, an assault on his dignity. As for the Metropolitan, its season and its immediate future depended on public acceptance of the tenor who had become the foundation of the opera company. Caruso would not have been the first idol of the world of entertainment who would have been destroyed by a hint of scandal. Worldly, sophisticated colleagues of Caruso had unanimously come to his defence, but there had been an undercurrent of real anger — noted in the local press — from a less well-educated part of the public over what was considered 'obscene' behaviour by the popular tenor. The extent of this anger would not be measured until the singer actually appeared on the stage, but there was no doubt that it existed, and that the incident had brought to the surface a smouldering hostility towards the 'dirty foreigners' who reputedly roamed the streets of New York in search of innocent, defenceless women.

For this reason, the night of 28 November, when the tenor was to make his first appearance of the season in New York, was of vital importance to both Caruso and the Metropolitan. The opera was *La Bohème*, and singing with Caruso would be Sembrich, a loyal friend and supporter, and Scotti, who had been at the tenor's side throughout his ordeal. These circumstances assured a friendly atmosphere on the stage, but the reaction in the auditorium remained in doubt. Not surprisingly, there had been extraordinary interest in the performance; in the hours preceding it, long lines had formed at the box office, with tickets being sold by speculators for three or four times their normal prices, as the merely curious joined the genuine opera-lovers in the clamour for seats. Inside the theatre, adding to the tension that pervaded the atmosphere, was a special detachment of twenty-five plainclothes policemen (the irony should have been noted) ready to maintain order in the event of a hostile demonstration.

There was no such demonstration. When the curtain rose on the Bohemians' Parisian garret, Caruso was already on stage, his back to the audience as he gazed out over the city's rooftops; Puccini's opera called for no grand entrance, which could set off an immediate demonstration — friendly or hostile. But when, a few anxious moments later, Caruso turned to face the audience, for the first time the public's verdict was unequivocal: the tenor was greeted with one of the most tremendous ovations in the history of the opera house. Caruso, overcome with emotion, seemed almost unable to go on; but, though singing somewhat tentatively at first, he and the other members of the cast concluded the first act in triumph. As the public roared its approval, Caruso and Sembrich were called before the curtain eight times. Each time the gracious soprano tried to leave the tenor alone so that he might enjoy a solo bow, but each time he clutched the sleeve of her dress, refusing to let her leave his side. Finally, on the ninth call, a smiling Sembrich managed to detach herself from her colleague, to the immense satis-

faction of the audience which proceeded to fill the house with cries of 'bravo'.

The following evening, Caruso quietly celebrated Thanksgiving with a few close friends at his hotel. He offered his own special thanks to all those who had steadfastly believed in his innocence and to the public which had loyally stood by him. Because of the pending appeal, however, the Monkey House Case was not completely closed. Further developments included the sudden appearance of the accuser, who claimed her name was Stanhope and not Graham, and who disappeared as suddenly as she had appeared, without having offered any substantial testimony. Then came the news of charges against the overzealous Patrolman Kane for making false affidavits in similar cases and the resignation from the force of Deputy Commissioner Mathot, who had been so active in prosecuting Caruso. Astonishingly, in spite of these developments, Caruso's appeal was rejected one month later.

The tenor wisely chose to let the matter rest there. He had been scarred by the ordeal and would never forget the humiliation he had needlessly suffered, yet he could take comfort in the knowledge that, no matter how unfairly he had been treated in the court and, at times, by the press, he had been thoroughly vindicated by his devoted public.

The remainder of Caruso's season was brilliant. Before the end of it, he had sung twelve roles, among them his first New York appearances in *Fedora* (at its American première), Meyerbeer's *L'Africaine* (which he had never sung before), and in the first Metropolitan productions of *Manon Lescaut* and *Madama Butterfly*. Puccini, on his first visit to New York, was present for the last two of these. 'Caruso was amazing,' the composer wrote to Sybil Seligman, following the première of *Manon Lescaut*, noting in another letter that he was 'singing like a god'. In yet another letter to Mrs Seligman, following the first performance of *Madama Butterfly*, he qualified his praise. 'As regards your *God* (*entre nous*),' he wrote, 'I make you a present of him — he won't learn anything, he's lazy, and he's too pleased with himself — all the same his voice is magnificent.'

Caruso had good reason to be pleased with himself. He had never let his public down and had finished the brilliant season in a blaze of glory, displaying astounding energy by singing seven performances between 13 and 23 March. He never disappointed Conried either, during what had been a difficult time in the managing director's life, personally and professionally. Conried had, for months, been suffering from a painful nerve disease and had feared, when the season opened, that this illness would rob him of the strength to carry out his tiring job. His task that season had been complicated not only by the possibly devastating consequences of the Monkey House Case, but also by the threat of a newly formed opera company which would offer direct competition to the supremacy of the Metropolitan among American opera companies.

The Caruso problem had been satisfactorily and rapidly resolved, but the challenge of this new opera company remained. The creation of the flamboyant showman, Oscar Hammerstein I, it was named the Manhattan Opera Company. Driven by a real passion for opera as well as by an intense hatred for Conried and the Metropolitan, the impresario had recruited, for his first season, some of the greatest stars of the world of opera — among them Melba, Calvé, and Alessandro Bonci, long Caruso's rival, whom Hammerstein felt would at least be able to hold his own in what was sure to be a well-publicized battle of the tenors.

Conried had good reason to worry: the Manhattan's first season was a resounding success, the critics singling out Melba and Calvé for special praise. Even more worrying was the critical acclaim for Hammerstein's production of *Rigoletto*, starring Melba and Bonci and the great French baritone Maurice Renaud, which the critic for the *New York Times* called 'the best seen in New York for many years'. This was a direct blow at the Metropolitan, where the Verdi opera, with Caruso, Sembrich and Scotti, had long been a favourite.

Bonci was Caruso's special irritant and, predictably, the press made much of the rivalry between the two men. The Metropolitan's star, however, was not unduly concerned — he had successfully faced such challenges before. Nonetheless, though Caruso was known for his extraordinary ability to get along with his colleagues, he made no secret of his contempt for Bonci.

This hostility certainly increased as New York's music critics lavishly praised the newcomer's performances and insisted upon making comparisons between the two singers; many noted that Bonci was a subtler artist,

OSCAR HAMMERSTEIN I, a brilliant, dynamic, and imaginative showman, who dreamed of building an opera company to challenge the supremacy of the Metropolitan.

lauding his phrasing and diction, though most conceded that the new tenor's voice lacked the richness and fullness of Caruso's. Comparisons, however, were useless. There was no real competition. Bonci excelled in the *bel canto* roles provided by the operas of Bellini, Rossini and Donizetti, most of which were not part of Caruso's repertoire. Furthermore, the Neapolitan tenor's hold on his audiences was secure — as long as he sang, there could be no rival as far as the public was concerned.

THE MANHATTAN OPERA HOUSE, on New York's West 34th Street, was built under Hammerstein's personal supervision to house the opera company he hoped might fulfil his dream.

In spite of this, Bonci was a thorn in the side of both Caruso and the Metropolitan; the only way to eliminate that thorn was to lure him away from the new company by offering him a higher salary, one Hammerstein, with far fewer resources at his command, could not match. By the end of the season, this had been accomplished and Bonci was eliminated as a challenge to Caruso. It was a double triumph for the Metropolitan, for Bonci, an excellent tenor, was sure to add to its lustre, and Conried, undoubtedly with Caruso's approval, could control his American career.

10
A
TRIUMPHANT
RETURN

C aruso had emerged unscathed from his encounters with San Francisco's earthquake and with New York's police and had successfully met Bonci's challenge. He was more secure than ever in his position as the world's best-loved tenor. If he had any fears concerning his reception in Europe following the Monkey House Case, they immediately proved to be groundless, for on his first appearance, at Covent Garden on the night of 15 May 1907, he was given a tremendous ovation. The British press had been outraged by the tenor's treatment at the hands of American justice, and the opera-going public clearly shared this indignation, greeting the tenor even more warmly than usual.

The season proceeded smoothly, with only one hint of scandal, which was quickly dispelled. During a curtain call which followed a performance of *La Bohème*, Caruso was seen blowing a kiss in the direction of a mysterious blonde, seated in an upper box. The identity of this woman was the subject of speculation the next day. Neither the press nor the audience at Covent Garden, apparently, had noticed that the kisses were meant for a small child, Caruso's three-year-old son Mimmi, attending his first Caruso performance, seated next to the unknown blonde, his governess, Miss Louise Saer, a most proper and serious Welsh lady, who was to look after the young boy conscientiously for twelve years and earn his lifelong devotion and gratitude. Caruso and Giachetti had settled their older child, Fofò, in a boarding school near

Florence, while Mimmi and Miss Saer spent most of their time in London, in a home set up for them by Caruso.

The tenor was relaxed and cheerful throughout the entire Covent Garden season. He was again playing jokes on his colleagues in the midst of performances, often to their amusement and sometimes to their discomfort and embarrassment. According to Sybil Seligman's son, Vincent, the management was none too pleased with their star tenor's playfulness, which offended those accustomed to the dignity and decorum of the opera house. Whether or not this was the case, Caruso's loyal public, who found nothing wrong with his behaviour at any time, was saddened to learn at the conclusion of the season that the tenor would not be returning to London in the near future. The reason given was money. Caruso had recently signed an exclusive four-year contract with Conried under which he would receive over $2,000 a performance, far more than the equivalent of the $1,200 paid to him at Covent Garden. This was the highest sum Covent Garden ever offered a tenor for a regular season performance, and Caruso might have accepted it, but under the terms of his new agreement, no decisions could be made without the consent of the managing director of the Metropolitan, who was unwilling to give that consent. After a two-month holiday divided between the Villa Bellosguardo and a home the tenor rented at the seaside resort of Viareggio, Caruso set off for Budapest for his début in the Hungarian capital, the first stop of a tour organized by his German manager, Emil Ledner. It was to be another one of his very few failures. During his first performance in *Aida*, the public was cool; the following day the critics were frigid. They reported that the tenor's poor performance was due to poor health, and they complained bitterly that he even refused to acknowledge the applause of the audience at the end of the opera. Caruso was furious, insisting that he was in perfect health and that he did not appear on stage to acknowledge his applause simply because the soprano — a little-known, last-minute substitute — refused to join him. He blamed the disastrous evening solely on the excessive prices charged by the management, which he felt turned the audience against him.

Ledner, of course, confirmed Caruso's version and angrily denied reports of the tenor's illness — being responsible for Caruso's future engagements, he feared that rumours of his poor health might adversely affect sales. He also blamed the management for charging inexcusably high prices for the Caruso performances. In his memoirs, written many years later, however, he confirmed that he was behind what had become known as the 'Budapest Legend', which blamed Caruso's Hungarian failure on the high prices charged by the management. The tenor was indeed, according to Ledner, far from his best on the night of the performance, having only recently recovered from a minor operation, performed in Milan, for the removal of small nodes on his larynx. His only excuse for not admitting the truth at the time was that news of this operation might well have had a disastrous influence on Caruso's career.

Caruso never returned to Budapest — it joined Naples, Barcelona, and San Francisco on his list of forbidden cities — but, to Ledner's relief, the tenor dispelled all doubts concerning his health by singing brilliantly during his next engagement, in Vienna, a few days later, and at subsequent performances in Leipzig, Hamburg, Frankfurt and Berlin.

Rumours of ill health conclusively proved to be false, and with the Monkey House Case behind him (his lawyer had sensibly abandoned plans for further appeals, feeling that the matter was best forgotten), Caruso made a triumphant return to America following his tour of Germany. He assured reporters that his one concern was the coming season at the Metropolitan, which was to start with the first New York production of *Adriana Lecouvreur*.

Hammerstein's Manhattan Opera remained a formidable challenge during that season. The energetic, imaginative impresario had gathered a star-filled company and an innovative repertory for the second year of his battle against the older, established house. His success during his first season could be attributed to the superb singing of Melba and Calvé and to his excellent productions of operas in the standard repertory. During the second season, he offered New York audiences an even greater array of stars and a number of seldom-heard operas, many of them French works neglected by the Metropolitan. Among the stars, making her American début, was the glamorous Scottish-born, American-raised soprano, Mary Garden, who had been the sensation of Paris and who had created the role of Melisande in Debussy's *Pelléas et Mélisande*, which she sang at its United States première at the Manhattan that season. Even

CARUSO AS LIONEL in Martha. *This role, which gave him a chance to display his flair for comedy, was one of his favourites until the middle years of his career, when he began to sing heavier roles.*

more dazzling was the sensational début at the new opera house of the coloratura Luisa Tetrazzini, fresh from her enormous triumph in London, who as Violetta took New York by storm in January 1908, and continued to draw packed houses whenever she sang.

For its part, the Metropolitan still offered New Yorkers some of the world's finest singers, but the older company could foresee problems. Sembrich and Emma Eames (an American, who often sang with Caruso), its two leading sopranos, were both close to retirement and would be greatly missed, though another soprano, Farrar, was beginning to attain that popularity with the American public which she would maintain for the rest of her career. Feodor Chaliapin's much-heralded first appearances at the Metropolitan proved to be disappointing,

*THE ROLE OF DES GRIEUX in
Massenet's* Manon *gave
Caruso an opportunity to
master the French style, and it
became one of his favourite
roles during the middle
period of his career.*

but, on the positive side, Bonci was singing superbly as was a Kentucky-born tenor, Riccardo Martin. In addition, the Metropolitan had a brilliant new conductor, Gustav Mahler, who shared the Wagner and Mozart repertory with another outstanding conductor, Alfred Hertz.

In spite of these considerable assets, the Metropolitan's most effective weapon in its war with Hammerstein was still Caruso. Singing in two out of every five of the company's performances, he completely dominated the season, during which he sang three roles for the first time. His opening-night performance of Maurizio in *Adriana Lecouvreur* was praised, though the opera itself failed to find favour with the public; his singing in Mascagni's *Iris*, too, was praised, but the role of a Japanese suitor proved difficult for him dramatically, and his Japanese costumes provoked laughter rather than the respect due to a Japanese nobleman. His Metropolitan début as Manrico in *Il Trovatore*, however, was an unqualified success, and his singing of the bravura aria, *Di Quella Pira* brought forth thunderous applause and insistent cries of encore. This appearance marked an important new phase in the tenor's career; it was recognition of a change in his voice, now more suited to heavier, heroic roles than it had been previously. As a result, he gradually began to abandon his lighter roles in *Rigoletto, Lucia*, and *Martha* — all three of which were entrusted to Bonci during the 1907–08 season.

The Metropolitan's complete dependence on its star tenor was looked upon with dismay by many observers of the New York operatic scene. Even good casts in popular operas did not guarantee large audiences — unless Caruso sang. As the critic for the New York *World* wrote: 'The season at the Metropolitan may be briefly summed up in one word — Caruso — for without this single artist I hardly see what would become of the season at all.' Commenting on the apparent decline of German opera, the conductor Alfred Hertz commented, 'I can't see that interest in Wagner is decreasing. Rather I find that the interest in M. Caruso is increasing . . . Go to the opera on Italian nights when that tenor is not singing, and you will find smaller audiences than on German nights.'

The 1907–08 season, the winter of Caruso's absolute supremacy, also marked the last year of the reign of Heinrich Conried. The managing director's health had continued to deteriorate, the company was losing money, and the initial successes of Hammerstein's Manhattan

Opera had forced the Metropolitan's board of directors to question the direction their own company was taking. In the middle of February, it was abruptly announced that Conried would be retiring at the end of that season, and shortly afterwards it was learned that both Toscanini and Gatti-Casazza would be leaving La Scala to join the New York company — Toscanini as chief conductor and Gatti-Casazza as managing director, sharing responsibility for that task with the German tenor Andreas Dippel, whose title would be administrative director.

The success Toscanini and Gatti-Casazza had enjoyed at La Scala, revitalizing Milan's great opera house, meant that the announcement of their appointment was greeted enthusiastically by New Yorkers who had never really taken Conried to their hearts. However, disturbing rumours soon began to circulate that Caruso, one of the few artists close to Conried and said to be on bad terms with Toscanini, would also be leaving the Metropolitan — to join Hammerstein's company. It was pointed out that the tenor's contract was with Conried, not with the Metropolitan, and that he was therefore under no further legal obligation to the company. His presence in the audience at several Manhattan Opera performances during the season inevitably increased speculation in the press.

Caruso quickly and decisively denied these rumours. It was true that he and the strong-willed Toscanini were not friends and had often disagreed. Nonetheless, Caruso had worked successfully with the fiery maestro in the past and had no intention of letting any disagreements with the conductor interfere with his own career at the Metropolitan. 'We have all received his reproofs,' the tenor told a reporter two years later, 'but none of us blame him. He is an artist in the highest sense of the word.'

As for his attendance at several performances at the rival opera house, these could easily be explained by his close friendship with Tetrazzini and his altogether normal curiosity to hear operas and singers unknown to him.

More important, although Caruso's contract did bind him directly to Conried, he felt a tremendous sense of loyalty to the Metropolitan. He was not, as was often pointed out, merely a member of the company; in many ways, he was the company, he enjoyed his position there and had no intention of abdicating. It was obvious to all who knew him that the Metropolitan was and would remain his home.

LUISA TETRAZZINI was one of the greatest of all coloratura sopranos. She first sang with Caruso in Russia in 1898. Though the two seldom performed together, they became close friends.

11
RIDI,
PAGLIACCIO

On 21 May 1908, Caruso left for Europe. He was unusually relaxed, determined that his summer would be a restful one. His plans included a benefit concert in London's Albert Hall, his first appearance at the Paris Opéra, a short visit to Naples to visit his ailing father, and, finally, a long reunion at his villa with Ada and their children.

After a few days at sea, the tenor's euphoria came to an end with the arrival of a cable announcing the death of his father. According to a friend who was travelling with him, Caruso collapsed when he received the news. He and his father had never been very close, but Caruso was an emotional man with close sentimental ties to his past, and now a part of that past was lost for ever. Once in London, the grief-stricken tenor went immediately to the home he had set up for Mimmi and Miss Saer. There, even more shattering news reached him: Ada, the mother of his children, with whom he had lived for twelve years, had run off with Cesare Romati, the family's young and handsome chauffeur.

Caruso was distraught but — according to some friends — not entirely surprised. He had, it seems, first learned of Ada's affair with the chauffeur while in America more than a year before. When the couple were reunited in Italy the previous summer, she had agreed to give up her lover, but the reconciliation was short-lived, and, after a few weeks together, Caruso had left for America again — without Ada.

Upon reflection, this final break was inevitable. The couple, once so much in love, had spent little time together in recent years. Much as Caruso professed his love for Ada, he had spent much of his time travelling. And Ada, though many years his senior, was still a beautiful and desirable woman, who had for the last few years chosen not to travel with him.

In spite of the steady deterioration of their relationship and Ada's abandonment, Caruso, still deeply in love, was crushed by her departure. Nevertheless, the same determination which had always characterized his approach to his career enabled him to put aside, temporarily at least, his profound grief in order to fulfil, after some hesitation, his commitment to sing in London on 30 May 1908. Though the audience was unaware of it, it was a painful personal experience for the distraught tenor.

As his part of the gala concert in aid of The League of Mercy, Caruso sang two solos: Tosti's *La Mia Canzone* and the heartrending and most appropriate *Vesti la Giubba* from *Pagliacci*. The audience was particularly moved by the *Pagliacci* selection, as were members of the press. The critic for the *Daily Mail* noted that the tenor had sung the aria with 'unmatched ease and brilliance', while the critic for the *Daily Telegraph* commented that 'the poignant despair with which he invested the words, *Ridi, pagliaccio, sul tuo amore infranto* (Laugh, clown, for the love that is ended), had a quite thrilling effect upon the audience.'

The distinguished audience, which included the King and Queen and the Prince and Princess of Wales, knew of the tenor's sadness at the death of his father, but only Tosti and Sybil Seligman, among those present, knew of the private pain which had gone into Caruso's rendition of the famous aria which expressed a clown's bitterness over his lover's betrayal. It is unlikely that this aria had ever before been sung with such profound conviction.

After enormous success in Paris, where he sang *Rigoletto* with Melba, Caruso was able to put his career aside and concentrate on his personal grief, devoting his time to making arrangements for his two sons, who were now motherless, and to a frantic effort to put together the pieces of his life, which would no longer include Ada Giachetti. His boys, with the aid of Miss Saer and Ada's sister Rina, who took over many of her sister's responsibilities, were well cared for. Caruso, however, was on his own and desperate. The man whose every move had been followed closely by the press suddenly disappeared from sight as he began his lonely crusade to understand what had happened and, perhaps, to convince Ada to return to him. No one knows exactly where he went during the early part of the summer, but apparently he spent most of his time travelling throughout France and England, with occasional stops at his villa. Martino, his valet, who was with him throughout the ordeal, reported later that he was so worried about Caruso's state of mind that while at Bellosguardo he slept outside his employer's bedroom, fearing that he might attempt to take his life.

Caruso, a private man though a public figure, was unwilling to display his grief in public. Instead, when he emerged from hiding in the middle of August, he responded to reports of Ada's elopement with a series of interviews in which he dismissed his grief, claiming, instead, that he was pleased that his union with her had

A MELANCHOLY CARUSO gazes at a photograph of Ada Giachetti, surrounded by photographs of their sons.

come to an end. She had not come up to his standards, he insisted, and he had no regrets. The next month, in an attempt to refute stories of his depression and his search for Ada (he emphatically told reporters she had never been his wife), Caruso turned up in Naples in a particularly ebullient mood. He was, he asserted, fresh from a pleasure trip to Tunis, where he had travelled in Arab costume in order to absorb local colour. Arriving in the city of his birth dressed in a flowing white kaftan, a turban wrapped around his head, he was delighted to be mistaken for a Turkish dignitary. Once he removed his disguise, he entered into Neapolitan life with a gusto quite obviously uncharacteristic of a pining lover. Quite the contrary. He was observed strolling along the city's waterfront, eating huge plates of pasta at seaside restaurants, and apparently enjoying himself immensely — in public, at least.

Most important for his own well-being, the tenor was gathering strength for the opera season to come. The loss of Ada was painful; the loss of his career would have been unbearable. Aware of this, Caruso travelled to Germany in late September to fulfil his first engagements of the new season. The brief tour, during which he was accompanied by his good friends Scotti and Farrar (both of whom sang with him), confirmed that his career had not suffered in the least, even after the turbulent summer. He was singing more brilliantly than ever.

When the tenor arrived in New York on 3 November 1908, some observers noted that he looked drawn and weary — the inevitable result, it was believed, of his emotionally exhausting summer. But he assured them he was ready for the new season, the first under the management of Gatti-Casazza and the first with Toscanini as chief conductor. The Italian press had complained that these two men had caught Caruso's all too contagious disease, *dollarite acuta*, but for New York audiences this disease was a blessing, as it was for the board of directors of the Metropolitan. It seemed certain that the newcomers plus Caruso, with the help of the brilliant conductors Mahler and Hertz, could successfully put an end to Hammerstein's challenge.

In spite of the new opera company's little publicized financial problems, that challenge was very much alive. The Manhattan season was a distinguished one, its success guaranteed by its three great sopranos, Melba, Garden and Tetrazzini and, again, by an imaginative repertory. Nonetheless, once more, that challenge was met successfully, largely by Caruso who remained as indifferent to the threat of the Manhattan as he was to the changes taking place at the Metropolitan. Conried was gone, and the tenor had his disagreements with Toscanini, but the real power at the opera house had fallen into the hands of Otto Kahn, the new chairman of the board of directors, and Kahn, a brilliant businessman and banker, as well as a gentleman of superb taste with a deep understanding of music, quickly became both a close friend of Caruso and an unfailing supporter.

Caruso certainly showed no signs of fatigue as he began the 1908–09 season with a display of energy which was unprecedented, even for him, singing in six of the company's first seven performances. It was an astounding record for a man said to be worn out after a disturbing summer. Following that *tour de force*, Caruso returned to a less hectic schedule, but, after singing his first New York Turiddu in *Cavalleria Rusticana* on 17 December, there was disturbing news: two performances were cancelled. The public was shocked, certain that something serious must have caused the indefatigable tenor to renounce his commitments. The official reason — strained vocal cords, caused by his superhuman activities at the start of the season — was plausible, but a rumour soon spread that the real cause was that the tenor was suffering from a far more serious illness that could actually threaten his entire career. Caruso angrily refuted the rumour as absolute nonsense, and his physician, Dr Holbrook Curtis, concurred, announcing that Caruso was being treated for nothing more threatening than a cold which had reached his vocal cords.

Predictions of dire tragedy were momentarily stilled when Caruso returned to the Metropolitan on 26 December to sing *Pagliacci*, and they were completely dismissed when, during the months of January and early February, he resumed his normal schedule, singing as splendidly as ever. Nonetheless, it was soon obvious that something was wrong. Following a performance in *Aida* on 13 February a few of the tenor's performances were cancelled, and, following a performance of *Manon* on 4 March, it was abruptly announced that he would be taking a month's rest. Once again, rumours of a serious throat ailment began to circulate. Although he insisted

THE YEAR 1908 *was not a happy
one for Caruso — his father
died and Ada Giachetti left
him — yet this caricature,
drawn in that year, shows
him well fed, elegantly
dressed, and apparently very
much in control of himself.*

publicly that he was merely in need of a rest from his heavy schedule, the tenor was privately both worried and frightened. On 2 April, after a month of inactivity, he wrote to his brother Giovanni: 'I will resume singing tomorrow matinée, and you can understand how nervous I am . . . Pray for me.'

Caruso did return to the stage the following day, met by an enormous crowd which greeted him with thunderous applause. Some of those present thought he looked haggard, but most reviewers felt his performance disproved all reports of a serious illness. In spite of this apparent recovery, however, it was clear to all who heard him during a performance of *Aida* only a few nights later that he was not at his best: his voice was heavy, and he was exercising uncommon caution as he sang. 'It was obvious that he needs a long rest,' a critic for the *New York Telegraph* wrote. 'He has somewhat overworked that frailest and most mysterious of musical instruments, the human voice, for years.'

Because of this and other similar appraisals of the tenor's latest performances, it should have come as no surprise when an official announcement was made that Caruso would not be joining the company on its annual American tour and that he would instead be returning to Italy in mid-April. Nonetheless, the public was stunned; this news seemed to confirm the gravity of his illness. These suspicions were intensified by a story in the *New York Times* of 14 April, which revealed that the tenor would be going directly to Milan where he would 'place himself under the care of an eminent specialist, in the hope that the climate and a series of operations will restore his throat to something like its normal condition.' In the same story, it was noted that a few years before Caruso had undergone surgery and had been warned to modify his busy schedule — a warning he had obviously ignored. 'His friends in this country, music lovers and opera goers,' the article concluded, 'are hoping that the fear that it is too late to save the voice is groundless.'

When Caruso boarded the *Mauritania* for Europe on 14 April, he responded angrily to the *Times'* story. 'The idea that I may never be able to sing again is ridiculous,' he told journalists. 'I assure my friends that the lapse is only temporary.' When asked where he would be spending the summer, he joked that he was going to visit Frau Wagner and study Wagnerian roles.

He was not joking, however, when he arrived in Liverpool in late April. Met by a throng of curious reporters, he insisted that his 'illness' had been an invention of the American press and repeated that there was nothing the matter with him that a badly needed rest could not cure. However, in spite of this denial, it was later learned that the tenor was, in fact, operated on in late May by a Milanese throat specialist, Professor Temistocle Della Vedova, for a removal of a nodular growth on the left vocal cord. At the same time that this news was leaked to the press — secrecy of any kind was almost impossible for a man of Caruso's immense fame — it was also confirmed that the tenor had undergone a similar operation, on the right vocal cord, a few years before.

According to the physician, the operation was a minor one, and a complete recovery could be expected after a short period of rest. To corroborate this optimistic prognosis, it was announced that the Metropolitan had extended his contract for three years beyond the present contract, which was due to expire in three years. Obviously, the New York company did not harbour any fears for the future of its star tenor.

In spite of this, Caruso was justifiably bitter over all the publicity concerning what he insisted was a minor operation. He had hoped that the operation might be performed in complete secrecy only because he felt that the seriousness of his illness would be exaggerated by the press, to the point of jeopardizing his career. Reports of his declining vocal powers were potentially damaging to his future; in fact, he had learned that these rumours had already influenced ticket sales for his tour of the British Isles later in the summer.

The rest of Caruso's summer and early autumn was devoted to a concerted effort to prove to the world that his recovery was complete. Three concerts were sold out in Ostende, while the British tour — which took him to Dublin, Plymouth, Blackpool, Glasgow, Edinburgh, Manchester, Belfast and Liverpool — and a hugely successful concert at London's Royal Albert Hall decisively proved the tenor's point, which was unequivocally confirmed by his first operatic appearances since his illness, in Germany, during the month of October. He was, once again, singing as only Caruso could. The Caruso fever, as the Germans called it, had become an epidemic, surfacing wherever he performed.

BLACK HAND DEATH THREAT FOR CARUSO

MAR 12 1910

Army of Police Guards Him as He Sings—$15,000 the Demand—Suspects Caught.

Guarded by as many police and plain-clothesmen as attend a President of the United States on his travels, Enrico Caruso made the trip in the Subway from his apartment in the Knickerbocker Hotel, Manhattan, to the Brooklyn Academy of Music on Monday evening, March 7, to sing the rôle of *Enzo Grimaldo* in "La Gioconda." It was his first public appearance since, on Friday, March 4, he had received a Black Hand letter demanding $15,000 or his life.

As Caruso sang—and he was in his best voice and sang without noticeable agita-tion—detectives kept guard over him in the wings and, in evening clothes watched the performance in the audience. Uni-formed policemen guarded the stage door and searched for suspicious-looking char-acters at all the approaches to the theater, and there were sleuths, disguised as Ital-ians, keeping a wary eye out in the gallery. In all, there were the Borough inspector, two police captains, several sergeants, twenty detectives, twelve mounted men and a large number of ordinary patrolmen stationed in or about the theater on the lookout for the blackmailers who sought to share in the profits of Caruso's golden voice. A large cordon of detectives surrounded the tenor on his way to and from the theater and did not cease vigilance until he was safely ensconced again in the rooms of his hotel.

But nothing happened.

The Academy of Music was packed to overflowing by an audience willing to un-dergo the risk of bomb-throwing for the privilege of hearing the greatest of tenors whose life the most desperate of blackmail-ing societies had menaced. Caruso was tumultuously applauded as he appeared. "Assassini! Assassini"!

"Base assassins! Base assassins"! By a curious coincidence, these were the first words that Caruso, as *Enzo*, had to sing, and as he sang them the applause broke out afresh.

Again, later, he sang: "We will save the innocent victim. * * (aside) I am dis-covered," and, in the third act, translated freely:

"The sharp axe for me is waiting:
Opens wide a dark abyss."

Perhaps there was special fervor in the tenor's voice and acting. At any rate, the audience seemed to find an extraordinary amount of realism in the situation.

Caruso did not like to talk of his troubles after the performance.

"I am not afraid," was all he would say; "but, certainly, the whole business is most unpleasant. Still, I am not afraid, for have I not always with me my pistols and my sword cane?"

Two persons were arrested Friday, March 4, charged with being suspicious persons and suspected of being implicated in sending the threatening letters to Caruso. They were Antonio Cincotta, forty-one years old, a Brooklyn saloonkeeper, and Antonio Misiani, an importer of wines, of Manhattan. According to the letter re-ceived by Caruso, the men had demanded that the $15,000 be placed in an envelope under the stoop of a factory at Van Brunt and Sackett streets, Brooklyn, and a decoy package was placed there. Misiani was bending over to reach for the package when something frightened him, and he fled with Cincotta and a third man, who escaped. The two who were caught were known to the police, who say that Cincotta had been twice arrested and acquitted of murder charges. When Misiani started to run he

How Caruso sang in Brooklyn Monday evening. Note the chorus of detectives.—*From the New York World.*

threw away a shotgun. The two were ar-raigned on Saturday and held in $1,500 bail for further examination.

Caruso received two threatening letters, both indicating that the writer was illit-erate. The first was addressed to him at the Metropolitan Opera House, where it was received March 1, and was translated as follows:

SIGNOR CARUSO: You to-morrow at the hour of two o'clock. You will be stopped by a boy and you must deliver $15,000. You think right not to say anything to nobody.
C. D. M.

Between the third and last letters of the signature, which is supposed to stand for Compagnia della Morte, "the Company of Death," there was a small cross about the size of the letters itself. The letter was postmarked Long Island City. Direc-tion was given to Caruso to turn the money over to the boy while walking along Forty-second street, and, with detectives in his wake, he did as instructed. He was not molested, however.

The second letter was postmarked Brook-lyn, March 3, and was translated thus:

"SIGNOR CARUSO: You yesterday went in company with two policemen. The boy couldn't make the salute. And you to-night must come to the house, hour of eleven. You must send in one bag the sum of $15,000, under the stairs where the factory is at the corner of Sackett and Van Brunt streets in Brooklyn. You think good and don't fail, and if you fail Saturday night will not pass that you will pay.
"LA M. N. C. D. M."

The signature is thought to stand for the Italian words meaning "the Black Hand, Company of Death."

THE BLACK HAND'S THREAT to Caruso's life was reported in great detail by the New York press. The threat was received on 4 March, and the tenor, heavily guarded, made his first appearance following it, in Brooklyn, on 7 March. This drawing shows a cartoonist's view of that performance. Note the chorus of detectives.

12
An ENCOUNTER
with the
BLACK HAND

The 1909–10 Metropolitan season, which opened on the night of 15 November with a performance of *La Gioconda* starring Caruso, Pasquale Amato, Emmy Destinn and Louise Homer, and conducted by Toscanini, was one of the most extraordinary in the history of the New York opera company or, for that matter, any opera company. Toscanini electrified audiences with a new production of *Tristan und Isolde* and, for the first time in New York, conducted performances of *Die Meistersinger* and Gluck's *Orfeo ed Euridice*, as well as an enormously successful production of *Otello*, which introduced the Austrian tenor, Leo Slezak, to New York audiences. Toscanini was not the only outstanding conductor of the season. Mahler led the first American production of Tchaikovsky's *Pique Dame* (with Destinn and Slezak), and Hertz's repertory included Wagner's *Ring* and Weber's *Der Freischütz*.

Obviously, this was not just another Caruso season, as critics had complained in the past — the new directors of the Metropolitan presented audiences with a brilliant array of artists in a marvellously diversified repertory of operas. Nonetheless, there was no doubt that the beloved Neapolitan tenor remained the company's single most important attraction. When he had arrived in New York, he had put to rest all talk about his illness at once. His voice was not only back to normal, but in some ways it was better than it had ever been. And that, he affirmed, would be his only comment about his health.

His performances in the course of the season demonstrated the truth of that statement. He no longer abused his voice, as he had in the past, but he sang nine different roles for a total of twenty-eight performances at the Metropolitan (plus fifteen performances in Brooklyn, Boston, Philadelphia and Baltimore, considered part of the company's regular season). Critics praised him unanimously, many noting a new artistic maturity and a greater musical refinement than before.

It was not only his voice and his increasingly effective theatrical presence that endeared him to the public. It was equally — as it had been from the beginning of his American career — his off-stage personality, his good nature and his unfailing generosity that set him apart from his distinguished colleagues. 'He is by all odds the most popular man who ever stepped inside the opera house as far as chorus members and other members of the institution are concerned,' an employee of the Metropolitan told a reporter, after the tenor had played Santa Claus to the entire company at Christmas.

Away from the opera house, too, Caruso showed his generosity by spending several hours each day answering his mail, much of which consisted of requests for financial help. He was a notoriously easy target for such requests, but not always, as he acknowledged during an interview in December 1909:

> One man write me his wife very sick. I send him five dollars. A few days later he say his daughter very sick. I send three dollars to him. When he says his son is sick, that's too much. I write and say I'm sick. I ask him if he wants me to build a hospital for his family. He make me very mad.

Caruso was even angrier when what had been an untroubled season was disrupted by an ugly note received on 1 March from the notorious Black Hand demanding a payment of $15,000 and threatening death if the payment was not received. The organization, associated with the Mafia, had for years been terrorizing prominent members of New York's Italian population with similar notes, and it was hardly surprising that the most famous Italian in America should receive one.

Caruso reacted defiantly. The note had asked that the money be given to a man who would stop him the

following day while on his way to the opera house; but instead of complying with these instructions, the tenor immediately notified the police who provided him with two bodyguards for his customary walk to work.

No one approached Caruso during his walk, but two days later another letter arrived, containing further threats and demanding that he leave the money in a bag by the entrance to a small factory in Brooklyn. This time, the still-defiant tenor, with the aid of the police, devised a more complicated trap. A decoy package, real money on top and counterfeit bills below, was given to Martino, his valet, who carried it to Brooklyn and, with plainclothes policemen watching from a distance, deposited it in front of the factory. Before long, three men arrived to claim the money; one managed to escape, but two, both of whom had police records, were arrested.

The arrests, however, did not put an end to Caruso's troubles. The police, fearing that other members of the Black Hand might seek revenge, insisted that he be placed under police protection, wherever he travelled and wherever he sang, for the remainder of his stay in the New York area. This was unnerving. Even more unnerving was the fact that in the next few months, the singer started to receive other copycat threats demanding money. Caruso, in public at least, stood firm in his defiance. He dutifully turned over each letter to the police and formally filed charges against the two men who had been arrested.

Though lauded for his courage in setting an example for other citizens who might be similarly threatened, a rumour began to circulate that the tenor had not been quite so courageous and that he had, in fact, made a payment of between $1,000 and $2,000 to the clandestine organization. This was neither confirmed nor denied, but it is significant that Caruso's signature was on a petition the following year for the early pardon of the two criminals who had been imprisoned because of his testimony.

Caruso managed to finish the Metropolitan season without showing any ill effects from yet another nerve-wracking episode. It was, all agreed, the most successful one of his career, but just as the public was delighted by the tenor's return to the top of his form and by the revitalization of the Metropolitan under Gatti-Casazza and Toscanini, it was also saddened to learn that 1910 would mark the end of Hammerstein's Manhattan Opera. The courageous, colourful impresario had continued to offer

CARUSO

'GREETINGS FROM DUBLIN', a postcard from Caruso to Tosti, dated 18 August 1909. The tenor was to give a concert at the Royal Theatre there on 20 August.

New Yorkers an exciting alternative to the Metropolitan, but he had overextended himself financially, speculating recklessly in real estate, and, as a result, was forced to abandon his operatic activities.

The annual tour of the Metropolitan, again New York's only major opera company, which began in Chicago on 4 April, was an extension of the company's brilliant New York season; but, on the road, even more than in New York, the principal, if not the only attraction, was Caruso. The tenor's fame had grown through the popularity of his recordings. In December 1909, he had signed a new agreement with Victor granting the company the exclusive right to make and sell recordings of his voice for a period of twenty-five years, and his name on a programme was, as always, a guarantee of a full house at all the company's stops on its tour around the United States.

This tour was a special one, for following the last American engagement in Atlanta, more than 200 members of the company set off for Paris, for the Metropolitan's first season abroad. A Paris season had been the dream of Otto Kahn who was anxious to show off his extraordinary American company to a European audience and had carefully planned an outstanding programme of Italian operas, conducted by Toscanini, for the occasion. The Parisian public would have a chance to hear Caruso in *Aida*, *Pagliacci* and *Manon Lescaut*; it would also be given the rare opportunity to hear Toscanini conduct Verdi's *Otello* and *Falstaff*, with brilliant casts that Kahn felt only the Metropolitan could assemble.

The season offered an embarrassment of riches, but, from the moment the programme was announced, it was clear that French opera goers were no different from their American counterparts: they clamoured for seats for Caruso performances but were slow to buy tickets for the performances of Verdi's late masterpieces. To

remedy this situation, it was decided that each purchase of a Caruso ticket carried with it the obligation to purchase a seat for *Otello* or *Falstaff*.

By the end of the Paris season, Kahn had achieved his goal: the Metropolitan was recognized as a major opera company by sceptical Europeans. However, it was Caruso who, once again, had carried the season, becoming this time the idol of the French public, not only because of his singing but also because of his behaviour away from the theatre. Curious crowds gathered in front of his hotel to follow his every move, and he acknowledged their interest with unfailing charm and grace. Autograph seekers flocked to his table at the Café de la Paix, where he usually lunched, and, never the inaccessible star, he responded warmly, appreciative of their attention. He became as well loved a figure in the French capital as he had become elsewhere.

These Parisian triumphs, unfortunately, were gained at the expense of the tenor's health. He had ignored his promises to his doctors and to himself to use his voice sparingly — he sang six times during his last eight days in the French capital — and was exhausted when he left. Fortunately, he had a chance during the summer to recover his strength. His plans included spending time with Mimmi, Tosti and the Seligmans in London, with other friends in Paris, and finally returning, at the end of July, with Mimmi and Miss Saer to the Villa Bellosguardo where they joined Fofò. This stay in Italy, however, afforded him little chance for relaxation. The villa was filled with painful reminders of the past. He realized that his sons, isolated from any contact with their mother, desperately needed maternal affection, and he learned that Ada Giachetti had instituted a lawsuit against him for defamation of character and had publicly accused him of stealing her jewellery (the case did not come to court for two years). The local press hounded him too. Italians, who had had little opportunity to hear him sing, were curious about the man who had brought so much glory to their country, and he had countless interviews focusing on the two issues most painful to him: his troubles with Ada, and the condition of his voice. This probing into his personal life upset him, but he fended off the questions with agility — he was used to them — and he consoled his Italian public by announcing that he would sing with the Metropolitan Opera Company in Rome the following year.

13
ILLNESS,
RECOVERY
and a
HUMILIATING
TRIAL

Caruso arrived in New York on 8 November 1910. The novelties of the new opera season were to be his appearances in the Metropolitan première of Gluck's seldom-performed *Armide* and in the world première of Puccini's *La Fanciulla del West*, based on a play by David Belasco and set in the American West. The Gluck opera, performed on the opening night, was conducted by Toscanini, and its cast included Fremstad, Amato and Homer. It was far from a typical Caruso opening, since his role, that of Renaud, a knight, was a small one compared to that of Fremstad, who sang the title role. Nonetheless, Caruso accepted this secondary role with enthusiasm, grateful for the chance to master a style to which he was unaccustomed. By accepting it rather than demanding a more showy role in a more familiar opera, he demonstrated once more that he was not just a superstar, but a serious and responsible musician who was willing to take chances.

Caruso spent most of the opening night in his dressing room — working on caricatures, a hobby since childhood at which he had become professionally competent — while his fellow artists sang on stage. One of these humorous sketches was a self-portrait of the tenor as Renaud, reclining on a sofa, eating a sandwich and fanning himself. His caption read: 'What I do in *Armide*'. He gave the drawing to a greatly amused Fremstad during an intermission.

During the next few weeks, the tenor returned to his more popular roles, but most of his energies went

into the preparations for the première of Puccini's new opera, *La Fanciulla del West*. Puccini and his publisher had passed him by when selecting a tenor to create the role of Cavaradossi in *Tosca*, but this time they were more than eager to have him in the cast of the first performance of the composer's latest opera, the first work by a living European to have its world première in New York.

It was Caruso's first chance to portray an American, Dick Johnson, a repentant outlaw, and he was intrigued by the challenge. Singing with him were Amato as Jack Rance, an evil sheriff, and Destinn, who was to sing the title role of Minnie, the golden-hearted but iron-willed girl of the Golden West. This 'American' opera was to be conducted by Toscanini, and the composer himself had come to New York to supervise the rehearsals. There were no Americans in charge to lend authenticity to the production, but, for the good of all concerned, Belasco, an impresario as well as a playwright, who had originally attended the rehearsals out of curiosity, soon took charge of the stage action.

It proved to be an exhausting task for Belasco, for it involved transforming a multi-national group of principals and an unwieldy chorus into a homogeneous and convincing collection of Western Americans. 'Men and women by the score and fifties would troop out on to the stage, range themselves in rows, and become merely a background for the principals,' he later recounted in his autobiography. 'Then for no purpose they would all begin to shrug their shoulders, grimace and gesticulate with their hands.' Caruso at first resisted Belasco's attempts to turn him into an American outlaw, but he finally gave in and delighted the director by learning, among other things, exactly how one should kiss a young lady in a bungalow during a blizzard.

When the opera had its première, it was a gala one in front of the most glamorous audience in the history of the Metropolitan — on the night of 10 December, both Belasco and Puccini were more than satisfied with the results of their efforts. Caruso, whose role was not a particularly gratifying one, appeared to enjoy the festivities immensely. At one curtain call, he playfully drew a revolver out of his holster; at his final one, he rubbed his neck, in mock pain, at the spot which had been touched by the rope which was to have been used for a thwarted lynching. And at the end of the evening he presented an emotional Puccini with a solid silver wreath, which had been designed by Tiffany, on behalf of the managing director of the Metropolitan.

Caruso sang the new opera, which never matched the popular success of the composer's earlier operas, eight more times that season. He sang brilliantly and seemed at his best as he resumed his standard repertoire, singing twenty times in a period of eight weeks. Because of this, it came as a shock when, following a performance in early February, it was announced that Caruso had to cancel four appearances. Though the public was again assured that the cause of the cancellations was simply a bad cold, rumours of a more serious illness, inevitably, began to circulate when the tenor suddenly left for Atlantic City for what was described as a complete rest.

CARUSO created surprisingly few new roles. He is seen here in one of them, that of Dick Johnson, in Puccini's La Fanciulla del West.

ILLNESS, RECOVERY *and a* HUMILIATING TRIAL

In spite of reassurances by Dr Curtis that the tenor would soon be returning to the Metropolitan, he did not appear on stage for the whole of March. Even more alarming, word that Caruso would rejoin the company during the last week of the season proved to be untrue. Instead, on 5 April, it was announced that he would soon be returning to Italy, to recover from his recent attack of influenza and laryngitis.

This news came as a devastating blow to the tenor's fans, confirming fears that his illness might have been a recurrence of the far more serious problems which had troubled him in the past; and the announcement that the Metropolitan's eagerly anticipated visit to Rome was also cancelled only added to the fears of the public. Though the long-term prognosis was said to be excellent, the immediate loss to the Metropolitan and to the opera-going public was considerable. 'There is no dispute that the temporary voicelessness of Enrico Caruso threatens somewhat to eclipse the gaiety of nations,' an editorial writer for the *New York Times* wrote on 21 April . . . 'If his voice does not return this summer, what can London do and Paris and Rome?'

London, Paris and Rome, it was soon obvious, would have to do without Caruso for a while. The tenor arrived in London in late April, determined that this time his visit there would really be the beginning of a long period of rest. He planned to lead a quiet, retiring life, visiting friends, shopping in the London stores which had always intrigued him, and, most important, spending time with his young son Mimmi. Yet a series of irritating problems, inevitable in view of his fame, once more prevented him from enjoying the peace he so desperately sought.

First, and most serious among these, was the persistent rumour that, because of his deteriorating health, his career was reaching its end. This story seemed to have been substantiated by a report from his Italian doctor, Della Vedova, who had declared that another operation to his throat would be necessary — an operation so serious this time that it could lead to the destruction of his vocal cords. Caruso was furious. He announced publicly that the Milanese doctor's declaration was nothing more than an effort to gain personal publicity and produced a statement from a notable English physician who affirmed that the tenor had been completely cured of the illness, a minor one, which had been troubling him.

IN THE CENTRE of this photograph is Arturo Toscanini, the dynamic, strong-willed conductor who conducted the world première of Puccini's La Fanciulla del West. *The composer is on the right, and, on the other side of the conductor, with his customary high collar, is David Belasco, whose 1905 play was the basis for the new opera, which was said to be the first grand opera to be written on an American theme. After the première, Puccini said, 'The performance has been perfect.'*

This constant need to combat stories of his poor health, which plagued him for many years, was not the only irritating problem which Caruso had to face while in England. Another concerned the home he had, a few years before, established for Mimmi and Miss Saer. Though obviously not his principal home, British authorities had, in the late spring of 1911, judged it to be his permanent residence and taxed him accordingly. The tenor, who had paid little attention to minor financial matters — he had more money than he could spend and what he had he spent generously — was outraged. Convinced that he had been treated unfairly, he reacted quickly and decisively, emptying the house of its contents and moving Mimmi and Miss Saer into the nearby home of Miss Saer's family.

Another irritant which served to disturb his peaceful summer was the news that he was being sued for $50,000 for breach of promise by the father of a young woman, Elsa Ganelli, for a short time his fiancée. The Ganellis

had in their possession sixty love letters from Caruso, adequate proof of at least a serious relationship. When the case came to court in Milan several months later, Caruso was, legally, if not morally, vindicated. Though he was censured by the judge for a 'morally deplorable act', and forced to pay all legal costs, it was ruled that a promise of marriage did not necessarily involve the obligation of marriage, and the claim for $50,000 in damages was dismissed.

Caruso felt wronged — by a publicity-hungry doctor, by the British authorities, and by the Ganellis (though he recognized his poor judgement in this case), but when he left London in June 1911 he was determined to put these irritations behind him and follow his doctor's orders.

He spent most of the summer in Italy, both at his villa and travelling around the country with his two sons. The complete rest ordered by his doctors was impossible — merely sitting in the sun was anathema to him, and although his doctors had recommended him to give up his incessant cigarette smoking he was unable to do so. Despite this, there was encouraging news throughout the summer about his health, from those who had seen him. A New York journalist who visited him at Bellosguardo reported that his voice was 'full, healthy, and jubilantly free'. The soprano Lillian Nordica heard the tenor sing in private and found his voice 'more beautiful than ever', and another of his colleagues, Riccardo Martin, told the press he had never seen Caruso looking so well or in such good spirits.

In spite of these optimistic assessments of his condition, considerable anxiety surrounded Caruso's next singing engagement, in Vienna in September, which would mark his first public stage appearances in over seven months. He had never before been absent from the theatre for such a long period. Happily for all concerned, however, that engagement justified the optimism expressed, and the tenor — performing in *Pagliacci*, *Rigoletto*, and *Carmen* — proved once again that he could sing as superbly as ever. The same could be said of his short German tour, which followed. His public in Germany, including the faithful Kaiser Wilhelm II, who came to hear him whenever possible, was elated at what seemed to be a confirmation of his complete recovery.

Nevertheless, his recovery was not as complete as it seemed to be, for at the end of the tour it was announced that Caruso had in fact been in poor health during the entire engagement, suffering from severe neuralgic headaches as well as occasional irritations of the throat. He had been urged by his physicians, his friends, and even the impresario, to cancel his scheduled performances, but he had been unwilling to disappoint the thousands of fans who had paid extravagant prices to hear him. At the very end, the truth became apparent. Though he had sung as brilliantly as ever while on the stage, during a farewell luncheon he suffered what was described in the press as a complete physical collapse. Once again, Caruso issued a denial: the 'collapse', he assured his public, was merely the result of the careless overuse of his voice after so many months of silence, and after boarding the ship for New York he sent the understandably nervous Gatti-Casazza a cable which read: 'My health is superlatively fine.'

By 1911, Caruso's fame was such that everyting he did or said was liable to be seen as being newsworthy. Reporters paid special attention to his physical well-being. If he injured his knee slightly, it was feared he might be crippled for life; if his voice showed the slightest sign of fatigue, word spread that he might never sing again. Nothing, however, could equal the coverage given to his romances — real, imagined, or, in many cases, inspired by overzealous press agents. It was not enough that he really was facing serious legal problems with Ada Giachetti, which would soon come to a head, and, to a far lesser degree, with Elsa Ganelli. To satisfy public curiosity, love affairs and 'engagements' had to be either exaggerated or simply invented.

The women involved included a Canadian singer, Lillian Grenville, who was at the time trying to make a name for herself at the Chicago Opera; the twenty-two-year-old daughter of a wealthy Argentinian, with whom Caruso had naively allowed himself to be photographed while they were both, separately, on holiday at the Italian resort of Salsomaggiore; a nineteen-year-old Sicilian peasant, for whom it was reported that he was willing to give up his career in exchange for the simple life of a farmer; and a wealthy American, Mildred Meffert, who had received and kept, it seems, a number of passionate love letters from the tenor. One story the press failed to report was that of the tenor's short but intense courtship of the spectacularly beautiful actress Billie Burke, who met Caruso in 1910 and described the relationship in her memoirs. 'He made love and ate spaghetti with equal skill and no inhibitions,' she wrote. 'He would propose marriage several times each evening.'

Because of this great interest in Caruso's love life, it is not surprising that the crowd of reporters who greeted him upon his arrival in New York on 8 November 1911, was less concerned with stories of his 'collapse' in Berlin than with rumours of yet another 'engagement', this time, to Emma Trentini, a fiery Italian soprano who had the year before created the title role in Victor Herbert's *Naughty Marietta*. Caruso vigorously denied these rumours. He had more important things on his mind, above all, the coming Metropolitan season, during which he would once again be put to the test to prove that he had not lost his voice.

He had no trouble passing this test. He sang thirty-eight times in New York and eleven times on tour, and, though he essayed no new roles, his first performance of *Manon* with Toscanini, on the night of 30 March, was considered one of the artistic high points of his career to date for its display of musicianship and refinement of style. It was a season notable for superlative performances and one undisturbed by scandals or startling revelations of any kind, and when Caruso left for Europe in early May he did so secure in the knowledge that he remained the undisputed King of Tenors, his title in no way threatened.

It was also a summer of splendid performances in Europe, in Paris, Vienna, Munich, Stuttgart and Berlin. Critics and public agreed that he sang superbly, particularly in Paris, where he was joined by the man considered the greatest of all baritones, Titta Ruffo. The two men had rarely sung together and, during the short Paris season, each stimulated the other with extraordinary results. The remarkable way in which their voices blended can still be heard on one joint recording, made in 1914, a shatteringly powerful interpretation of the duet which closes the second act of *Otello*. In their Paris appearances (not, unfortunately, in *Otello* which Caruso never sang on stage), these two great singers both emerged triumphant. Their friendly battle for vocal superiority was an attraction for the public; but although Ruffo was frequently called the 'Caruso of baritones', Caruso was never labelled the 'Ruffo of tenors'.

Caruso could take satisfaction in his continuing supremacy and in the prevailing critical opinion that he was the equal of, or even better, than the Caruso of old. This pleasure, however, was not an unmitigated one, for before returning to the Metropolitan in the autumn of 1912, he had to endure the most emotionally shattering episode of his life, a widely publicized trial in a Milanese courtroom, which finally settled his differences with Ada Giachetti.

The Monkey House Case, the Ganelli suit, and the many reports of his impetuous involvements with a number of women were all embarrassing incidents, damaging to the tenor's pride and innate dignity. But the Giachetti trial was something far more serious, a bitter public airing of his relationship with the mother of his children, a woman many of his friends would continue to think of as the only real love of his life.

Ironically, there would have been no trial had it not been for Caruso's insistence upon a more than complete vindication of charges brought against him earlier by the soprano. These accusations had first been made in the pages of one of Milan's most distinguished newspapers. According to Giachetti, who insisted that Romati the chauffeur had not become her lover until after her relationship with Caruso had come to an end, the tenor had done everything in his power to ruin her career. He had made defamatory statements about her and had seen to it that all letters sent to her from America were intercepted and delivered to him, among them one which contained a contract to sing at Hammerstein's Manhattan Opera House. In addition, she charged that Caruso had stolen from her thousands of dollars' worth of jewellery and all her theatrical costumes.

With public opinion on her side as a result of these newspaper articles, the soprano followed up her accusations by formally filing suit against Caruso, a suit which, after several months' investigation and the cross-examination of almost one hundred witnesses, was dismissed by the public prosecutor. Caruso was held blameless of any wrong-doing and, thus, publicly vindicated. But this was not enough for the embittered tenor. Feeling the need to pursue the matter even further, he filed a countersuit against Giachetti, charging her with defamation of character.

Proceedings began on 25 October 1912, and continued for four days. Caruso was present throughout the hearings, but Giachetti remained in South America where she was performing with an Italian opera company.

The tenor and his attorneys carefully countered each of the soprano's charges. They produced letters from Giachetti which proved that the affair with Romati had begun long before her relationship with Caruso had come to an end; they offered evidence in the form of a statement from Hammerstein that the Manhattan Opera Company had never offered her a contract; and, in answer to the charge of theft, they produced a letter from Giachetti in which she promised Caruso that she would return to him all jewellery, letters and other effects.

Testimony was bitter from both sides, and Caruso was visibly moved as the story of his betrayal was recounted to the court. He himself gave an emotional account of his life with Giachetti and how it had changed after ten years of what seemed to be perfect happiness. Several witnesses told of the soprano's passionate, unreasonable attachment to Romati; others spoke of Caruso's unfailing love and generosity towards her during their years together. When one witness told the court that Giachetti never loved the tenor, not even during the first years of their life together, and offered to show proof, the tenor covered his face with his hands and sobbed.

At the end of the trial, Giachetti was found guilty and sentenced to one year in jail, a sentence she never served, since she never returned to Italy. Caruso had been absolved of all wrong-doing and had behaved himself properly and with dignity throughout the hearing. Yet the experience had been deeply humiliating. As one Italian journalist noted, 'The revelation to the stunned world of his misfortunes caused more pain to the sensitive Caruso than did the sentence to the others.'

Caruso and Giachetti were never reconciled, though they secretly met again and the tenor continued to send her a monthly allowance until the end of his life. Emil Ledner, who had been with him throughout the trial, commented: 'Giachetti was removed from personal contact with Caruso, but not from his life. She was never out of his thoughts, his inner life, his feelings — perhaps as long as he lived.' Their two children never again saw their mother. A portrait of her, in the belvedere of the Villa Bellosguardo, was stored in the villa's attic. Fofò, the elder son, understood, but Mimmi was puzzled. He was fascinated by the painting, but each time that he asked who the woman was, he was told that it was none of his business.

14
'STILL
SUPREME'

When Caruso left for America in late October 1912, he was determined to devote himself single-mindedly to his work. While he realized that his private life was of legitimate interest to his public — this was a price of fame — he hoped that his accomplishments as an artist might completely overshadow his personal difficulties.

Over the next few years, his artistic achievements were spectacular. There were high points and occasional low points, but for the most part it can simply be stated that the tenor performed superbly.

Throughout the 1912–13 Metropolitan season, Caruso was in excellent voice, singing ten different roles and averaging two performances a week. He continued to have a remarkable ability to get along with his colleagues, displaying a rare sensitivity to their needs during a performance. One example was noted on the season's opening night, when he sang the role of Des Grieux in *Manon Lescaut* opposite the twenty-five-year-old Spanish soprano, Lucrezia Bori, who was making her American début. It was a somewhat disappointing beginning — perhaps because of Caruso's dominating presence in the cast, according to some listeners. 'Mixed with the rich organ tones of Signor Caruso, her voice seems pallid and infantile', the critic for the *New York Tribune* wrote of her singing during the first act. Although the same critic felt that Bori, later a great popular favourite, improved in the second act, he noted that Caruso 'seemed purposely to have modified his own glorious tones for her sake.'

This might well have been the case. Caruso, given his position as a superstar, could well have monopolized the stage, ignoring other members of the cast and singing directly to his adoring public, but he was too much the musician, ever aware that he was part of an ensemble, to do so. Though often a prankster on stage, he played jokes only on friends or on other experienced singers, like Scotti, Melba or Destinn, and never on young, inexperienced artists, whom he unfailingly helped and supported. After his death, his close friend, Marcella Sembrich told reporters: 'He was courteous to his associates, so generous to all. Also he had that inborn instinct of the true artist — the desire to aid someone else to be as great or a greater singer than he was himself.'

Caruso returned to Europe in May 1913. His first engagement was in London, where he was to sing at Covent Garden for the first time in several years. Shortly after his arrival in London he was irritated to read an extraordinary analysis of his vocal skills, given to the press by a British physician, Dr William Lloyd. According to Lloyd, the tenor's success as a singer could be accounted for by his unusual physical characteristics, above all the structure of what he called 'his entire throat machinery'. Moreover, the doctor found that Caruso had music in his bones, that the simple tapping of the Caruso knuckles resulted in a vibration that was higher and more resonant than that produced by tapping the knuckles of an ordinary mortal. He was, one headline writer concluded, a 'one-man band'.

Caruso was angered by this absurd representation of himself as a freak of nature. He was tired of writers trying to account for his extraordinary talent by bizzare diagnoses of his throat, his chest, his lungs and his vocal cords. He was, above all, an artist and a musician, with an admittedly remarkable voice. When asked how he produced his ringing top notes, he had a simple explanation: 'From G on up I poosh!'

His return to Covent Garden had been eagerly anticipated. Even at twice the prices ordinarily charged, tickets for the evening of his return — in *Pagliacci* on 20 May 1913 — had been sold out for weeks, and queues for unreserved gallery seats began to form at 5.45 on the morning of the performance.

This return to the scene of so many earlier triumphs proved a surprisingly unnerving experience. As the performance began, Caruso was even more tense than usual — for the first time in his career, he feared unfavourable comparisons with his earlier performances. For a few moments, his voice was unsteady, but he quickly recovered and delighted his public by singing with the brilliance they had remembered. His fears had been groundless. Nevertheless, at the end of the first act, the strain took its toll. Following a few enthusiastic curtain calls, he fell into a dead faint — happily, out of the view of the audience, which never guessed what had happened. Carried back to his dressing room, he managed to regain his composure and concluded the evening in triumph.

There were no signs of any strain in the course of his later performances. On the contrary, many critics noted his improvement as an actor as well as a vocal artist. Without a doubt, the highlight of the season took place on the night of 23 June, when 'at the King's request', and in the presence of King George V, Caruso and Melba, after many years, performed in their earliest success, *La Bohème*. Osbert Sitwell, who was in the audience, described the two (Melba was fifty-two years old and Caruso forty) as 'fat as two elderly thrushes, trilling at each other over the wedge of tiaras', but he confessed that Caruso's voice carried 'the warm breath of southern evenings in an orange grove, and of roses caught in the hush of dusk at the water's edge.' The audience had no reservations whatsoever, and so overwhelming was the success of that evening that a repeat performance was arranged for the night of 28 June, Caruso's last appearance of the season.

When, after a two-month rest at Bellosguardo, the tenor resumed his schedule, he travelled to Vienna, Munich, Stuttgart and Hamburg. Though some critics complained that he was not always at his best (he had been suffering painful headaches, which had at times caused him considerable discomfort while on stage), the German-speaking public was as Caruso-mad as ever; in their opinion their idol could do no wrong.

The same could be said of the New York audiences which cheered him during his next season at the Metropolitan, another season free of scandal and controversy, and, apparently, of the headaches that had previously beset him. There was one novelty that season for Caruso, the first Metropolitan performances of Gustave Charpentier's *Julien*, a sequel to the composer's successful *Louise*, which

CARUSO AS HE SAW HIMSELF in the title role of Julien in Gustave Charpentier's 1913 sequel to his successful opera, Louise, written in 1900. Julien was first performed at the Metropolitan in 1913 and was a dismal failure. The role was one the tenor should never have undertaken.

had first been produced in Paris in 1900 but had still not been given at the Metropolitan. Caruso had studied the role of the protagonist carefully during the previous summer, and the composer himself had enthusiastically approved the tenor's interpretation when he ran through it for him during a meeting in Berlin in October. Unfortunately, the result was not worth all the effort Caruso had put into learning a complex role. Farrar, his co-star at the première on 26 February 1914, pronounced the opera a 'wild and confusing hodgepodge', and neither the press nor the public were inclined to disagree. *Julien* was performed five times that season at the Metropolitan and never again. Farrar noted: 'At least there was never talk of revival, thanks be!'

Caruso's year was enlivened by an incident which has become an essential part of the Caruso legend — the first and only time he sang an aria intended for a bass. The occasion was a performance of *La Bohème* in Philadelphia on the night of 23 December 1913. That day, before the performance, the tenor had lunch at Del Pezzo on 34th Street, his favourite restaurant in New York, with his good friend Andres de Segurola, who was scheduled to sing the bass role of Colline in Puccini's opera. During the meal, Caruso noticed that his friend's voice was hoarse and learned that de Segurola feared he might be unable to fulfil his commitment. Later that day, on the train to Philadelphia, de Segurola tested his voice and was alarmed to find that it was even worse than it had been at lunch. He turned to the tenor for help, and Caruso suggested that he use his voice sparingly until the last act, at which time he, Caruso, would if necessary substitute for him in singing the important aria *Vecchia Zimarra*.

De Segurola followed his friend's advice; for three acts, he spoke his part. When he reached the famous coat song in the opera's fourth act, he realized, to his horror, that his voice was completely gone. Caruso, noting his colleague's panic, whispered, 'How do you feel?' and the bass answered, 'Terrible.' There was no time to lose, and to the astonishment of the conductor, Giorgio Polacco, Caruso sang the well-known bass aria, pulling de Segurola to his side so that the audience would not realize what had happened. From all accounts, he sang the aria magnificently — though when he finished it he was trembling and later confided that he had never been so nervous on the stage. The audience was unaware of the

CARUSO

ruse. Caruso later recorded the aria, which he presented to the principals; he did not want the recording to be released commercially, however, despite the urgings of some of his friends. 'I am not a basso,' he said. 'Why I should then put my good friend Chaliapin out of business?' (The recording has, however, since become available.)

In 1914, once again, Caruso's first European engagement was at Covent Garden. It was a flawless season. After his first performance, in *Aida*, the critic for the *Pall Mall Gazette* wrote: 'There is no dramatic tenor like him . . . In short, he is still supreme in Italian opera.' Each successive appearance drew similar praise. No performance, however, was greeted more enthusiastically than was his final one, on the night of 29 June, in *Tosca*. 'So packed was Covent Garden last evening, and so eager were all in the crowded audience to make the very most of their opportunities to the way of paying tributes to the "hero" — in every sense — of the occasion that it might almost have been Caruso's farewell to public life, and not merely his last appearance this season,' wrote the critic for the *Daily Telegraph*.

Ironically, though neither he nor his public could have known it, that performance was, indeed, the tenor's last appearance in London. The farewell appearances of singers and other entertainers of Caruso's stature are generally carefully planned, gala occasions — emotionally charged and sentimental — but it was to be Caruso's fate that there would never be any farewells for him. Without planning them, and without fanfare, he had already said his goodbyes to Vienna and to Germany, just as he was saying goodbye to his adoring London public, one of the first to champion and to cherish him.

On 28 June 1914, the day before Caruso's last performance in London, Archduke Francis Joseph Ferdinand of Austria and his wife were assassinated at Sarajevo by a Bosnian revolutionary. This event was to trigger the First World War and to change the course of Caruso's life.

Fresh from his triumphs over the past several months, he was again in desperate need not only of a rest, but also, even more important, a quiet period away from the public eye. According to the many doctors he had consulted, the painful headaches he had suffered periodically might well have been caused by the emotional strain of the past few years, compounded by his never-ending efforts to please his public. He felt a tremendous loyalty to that public,

ANTONIO SCOTTI, *shown in one of his greatest roles, that of Scarpia in* Tosca. *It was in this role that he made his début both in London and in New York.*

but he also began to look forward to the day when he could end his hectic life. 'If I had known the high price of celebrity,' he wrote to a friend in Naples, 'I would have gladly become a member of the chorus. For three years I have suffered from headaches . . . and I don't know what to do, since I no longer belong to myself.'

Throughout the summer and early autumn, the war spread throughout Europe; most of the continent was involved in a bloody struggle. As a result, the tenor's planned tour of Germany was cancelled, allowing him to accept an urgent invitation to sing at Rome's Teatro Costanzi on the night of 19 October. The special performance of *Pagliacci* had been hastily arranged, and it was announced that Caruso had agreed to participate because of a 'high sense of patriotism' — proceeds were to be used to aid Italian emigrants who had been forced by the war to return to their homes.

This announcement was not greeted with unqualified enthusiasm. For many Italians, the tenor had betrayed his own country early in his career, surrendering to the temptations of the American dollar. Indeed, he had not sung in his native land for more than ten years. One journalist indignantly accused him of not being a real Italian, of having forgotten his own country and advised him to give up his rights as an Italian citizen and face the fact that he had become an American.

These charges were rebutted by Caruso. He proudly reaffirmed his allegiance to his native land and declared that he would join the Italian army if called upon to do so. (Emma Trentini, when asked to comment, stated that the man she once declared to be her fiancé was too fat to fight, but that he might serve his country as a cook.) He assured reporters that only the demands of his career had led him to spend most of his time away from Italy. He might have added that he was only one of very many Italian and other European singers who spent most of their professional lives in either North or South America, because the pay was considerably higher in such cities as New York or Buenos Aires.

Despite any resentment that might have been harboured towards him, Caruso's appearance on an Italian stage after so many years was greeted with thunderous applause; the audience clearly did not agree with those who had attacked him. The performance, in every way a gala one, conducted by Toscanini, was an unqualified success. The

THE HMS CANOPIC left war-torn Europe on 14 October 1914. Among its passengers were Caruso, wearing a beret, in the second row; Gatti-Casazza, wearing a grey hat and coat and standing behind Caruso; and Toscanini, to the impresario's left. Lucrezia Bori stands in the middle of the back row.

next day, the critics were unanimously enthusiastic; even those critics who were sceptical of his immense worldwide reputation were convinced by his masterful interpretation of the role of Canio.

Following this unexpectedly gratifying reception in his own country, the tenor embarked from Naples on the HMSS *Canopic* for New York — to the delight of his American public who had feared he might become a victim of the European war.

The late summer and autumn of 1914 had presented complicated problems to the management of the Metropolitan anxious to see to it that their singers, scattered throughout Europe, would somehow be able to fulfil their engagements in America. Gatti-Casazza, Kahn and other officials of the company had worked tirelessly to

arrange this difficult exodus. Not only did they have to establish the whereabouts of the singers; they also had to deal with the delicate problem of arranging a complex schedule of sailings, since various nationalities objected to the presence on their ships of singers who had pledged their allegiance to hostile nations.

Fortunately, the red tape was kept to a minimum, and the countries involved proved to be co-operative, all apparently, anxious to have their culture represented in America. Nonetheless, it was with considerable relief that Gatti-Casazza was able to notify Otto Kahn in New York in late October that the *Canopic* had sailed from Naples, and that Caruso, Farrar, Bori, Hempel and Destinn were among its passengers, thus assuring a season of opera at the Metropolitan.

15
A
DRAMATIC TENOR

For many years, the Metropolitan had been one of the world's leading opera houses. The New York company's financial resources as well as its singers, its productions, and its sometimes adventurous programming could be equalled by few other companies in the world. In 1914, as the new season was to begin, it was without a serious rival anywhere, both because of the restrictions imposed by the war in Europe and because of the ingenuity of the Metropolitan's directors in bringing together in America many of the world's greatest singers.

The undisputed star remained Caruso. His own assessment of his singing, following his opening-night performance in *Un Ballo in Maschera* was 'better than ever'. It was an opinion to be taken seriously because the tenor was known for his candid and often severe criticisms of his own performances. Many of these opinions were jotted down and can be found among his scrapbooks. For example, following a 1914 performance of *Manon*, a critic had written that 'neither Caruso nor Farrar were vocally at their best'. The tenor cut out the review and pasted it in his scrapbook, with the word 'liar' written over it. Furthermore, many of the vouchers which accompanied the cheques received for his performances also contain his personal appraisals: they run the gamut from 'fair' to 'good' to 'marvellous'.

Certainly those who heard the tenor sing throughout that season would have written 'magnificent' or at least 'very good' in their programmes. He was singing brilliantly,

and when an official announcement was made in late January that he would be leaving for Europe in February, two months before the end of the Metropolitan season, the New York public was stunned, fearing once again that he was suffering from serious vocal problems that might necessitate another operation. The truth, however, was far less alarming. Caruso was leaving New York to keep a promise made several years before to Raoul Gunsbourg of the Monte Carlo Opéra — one of the first men to help him to achieve international fame — that he would spend one more season at the jewel-like opera house. Because of the war, Gunsbourg desperately needed Caruso's presence in his company at that time to stimulate tourism, and Caruso, out of loyalty, responded to that need.

The Monte Carlo engagement, as expected, was another splendid success. But, before it, Caruso had once again worried, as he had on his return to Covent Garden, that the public might find that his voice had lost some of its remembered freshness for he had not sung at Monte Carlo since 1904. Furthermore, he complained to one journalist that audiences demanded perfection from him and that

CARUSO FIRST SANG the demanding role of Riccardo in Verdi's Un Ballo in Maschera *during his second visit to St Petersburg. Following one performance in the role at Covent Garden, a critic for the* Daily Telegraph *wrote that he 'lifted his listeners to the supreme heights of dramatic enjoyment'.*

these high expectations, as well as the high prices charged to hear him sing, no longer permitted him the occasional, and inevitable, off-night allowed any other singer.

After Monte Carlo, Caruso was again faced with the challenge of singing before audiences that had not heard him sing for many years — since 1903, in this case — when he agreed to join an Italian opera company on an extended tour of South America. As before, he easily met the challenge, singing fifty-two performances in 104 days, a stupendous feat. Three occasions were of special interest in the course of this extraordinary tour. On 18 June he agreed to replace the baritone Giuseppe Danese, who showed up at the theatre practically voiceless, in singing the Prologue to *Pagliacci*. This time, unlike his Philadelphia Colline, the audience had been informed of the substitution, and the tenor took twenty-five curtain calls following what must have been a remarkable interpretation of the well-known prologue, written for a baritone. On another occasion he sang for the first time on the operatic stage with the coloratura soprano Amelia Galli-Curci; their performances of *Lucia di Lammermoor* which they sang only twice, made operatic history at Buenos Aires' Teatro Colón. On the third occasion, the night of 4 August, he again sang with Titta Ruffo, in *Pagliacci*, one of the very few performances that featured these two great singers.

Following this long and immensely successful tour, Caruso planned to return to Italy to enjoy a period of uninterrupted rest at the Villa Bellosguardo. However, even before arriving there he received an urgent plea from Toscanini to take part in two benefit performances of *Pagliacci* at Milan's Teatro Dal Verme. Unable to refuse, he agreed to cut short his holiday and return to the city of some of his earliest triumphs at the end of September, before returning to New York.

Of all Caruso's unplanned farewell performances, none would have pained him more than these last appearances in his native country. This time, his fear of being unfavourably compared to his younger self almost paralysed him, as he prepared for his first entrance. Armand Crabbé, the Belgian baritone who was part of the cast, noted in his memoirs: 'When he made his entrance in the circus wagon he had to be supported as his knees were knocking under him. On seeing this pitiable sight, I thought of the Caruso of yesterday, so sure of himself, so full of fire and virile youth . . .'

In spite of this uncertain beginning, the tenor sang
not only with enough 'fire and virile youth' to delight
the huge audience which filled the theatre; he also dis-
played a maturity which several of the critics noted with
admiration. The director of the *Gazzetta dei Teatri* wrote:

> The great artist is no longer the aria singer, no longer
> the 'furtive tear' which delights those who hear him.
> It is the bitter weeping, the heartrending sobbing, the
> sorrowful spasm which springs from his eyes, which
> chokes his throat and which bursts forth from his chest
> . . . People scream, shout, applaud, go into raptures,
> and no one regrets having paid so much for that hour
> of fantastic pleasure of the intellect and of the soul.

This maturity was also noted by the reviewer for *L'Illus-
trazione*:

> Once he was a refined tenor, a '*tenore di grazia*' a kind
> of Gayarré; today he has become a dramatic tenor. His
> voice has lost its former sweetness, but it is now armed
> with a new, impassioned vigour . . . Before us was not
> only a great singer, but also a great actor . . .

This inevitable change in Caruso's voice was obvious
to New York critics following the opening of the Metropolitan's 1915–16 season. The work performed, on 15
November, was Saint-Saëns' *Samson et Dalila*, not heard
at the opera house since 1895, and the tenor's assumption
of the heavy, dramatic role of Samson marked a decisive
turning point in his career, his emergence as a true dramatic tenor. It was, for Oscar Thompson, a respected
critic, the end of his 'raw beef' period. Reviewing Caruso's
career, Thompson wrote:

> The voice in these last years showed wear. Upper tones
> were not infrequently jagged and had lost something of
> their vitality. The middle and lower register . . . were
> dark and baritonal when power was applied, though
> still sumptuously beautiful . . . His style frequently
> suggested his earlier years in its lyric grace, but there
> was now greater artistry and far more intellect in the
> singing. Only in the *mezza voce* was it as entrancing
> in sheer sound, but his art had gained in restraint and
> taste what his tone had lost in sensuous appeal.

THE ROLE OF SAMSON in Saint-Saëns' Samson et Dalila, which Caruso sang for the first time on the opening night of the Metropolitan's 1915–16 season, marked a turning point in the tenor's career. That night he was able to prove that he had made the transition from lyric to dramatic tenor.

Caruso's Samson was not one of his most popular roles. The public clamoured to hear him sing in those operas which had earned him his early fame, and in spite of his reluctance to continue singing at least one of them — the Duke in *Rigoletto* — he obliged throughout the season.

Undoubtedly the most colourful performance of the season took place on the night of 17 February 1916, when Caruso sang in *Carmen*, opposite Geraldine Farrar. The beautiful Farrar had spent the previous summer in Hollywood, making a film of *Carmen*, and for her first appearance in the role at the Metropolitan that season, she was determined to apply some of the techniques learned while in the film capital. Her performance was, at the very least, a prime example of theatrical hysteria. During the first act, she enthusiastically beat one of the cigarette girls, throwing her to the ground and then pummelling her. In her third-act struggle with Caruso, she slapped and bit the startled tenor — according to Frances Alda, who was singing the role of Micaela, she actually drew blood. Caruso was furious. He admired and respected Farrar as an artist and as a friend, and he had certainly played his share of tricks on his fellow performers when on stage. This uncalled-for display of realism, however, was too much for him. He retaliated by brutally pushing the soprano to the ground; Farrar landed with such a thud that members of the startled audience gasped. At the end of the performance, angry words were exchanged between the two stars. Caruso reportedly told her that she should remember she was not in the movies, but on the stage of the Metropolitan, to which Farrar replied that if he did not like her Carmen, he should get someone else to play the role the next time. No, the tenor retorted; another such scene could be avoided by getting another Don José.

The New York press had a field-day the following morning. Farrar was, according to the *Sun*, 'a muscular Carmen'. The *Tribune* labelled her a 'very rough Carmen'. Critics agreed that the soprano had sung poorly, while Caruso was at his best. The opera house's management, instead of capitalizing on the publicity, did its best to minimize the conflict, and the principals gave out conciliatory statements. Caruso said:

> I am a singer, not a fighter. Sometimes families squabble, often somebody says something on the stage which must not be told outside the theatre. What occurs behind the stage — that is our business. What occurs on the stage — that is for the public.

Farrar maintained that the two singers were still good friends, and Gatti insisted that there were no problems at all between the two stars.

Whatever had happened behind the scenes that night, there were no problems when the two singers again appeared in *Carmen* eight days later. The crowd that filled the theatre, hoping for another dramatic encounter, was disappointed. There was no slapping and no biting, and the result was a far more convincing performance. The audience burst into laughter when, after the 'Flower Song', the couple embraced far more affectionately than usual — signifying the end to their short-lived conflict.

16
The
PATRIOT

C aruso's New York season had been of great importance artistically, but he had not been in perfect health. The painful headaches from which he had suffered periodically had recurred, and he had even, secretly, undergone minor surgery at the hands of Dr Curtis who believed this time that the trouble was caused by nothing more serious than a nasal infection. The surgery, however, had not helped, nor had the intensive massage treatments prescribed by the doctor. Because of this, he looked forward to a peaceful summer in Italy, and, with European opera houses closed because of the war and no engagements scheduled until the autumn, Caruso was able to enjoy just such a summer. Nonetheless, he was, as always, preoccupied with his work, even while at his villa, and he drove himself with his customary energy in an effort to prove to New York audiences in the autumn that his growth as an artist had more than compensated for the loss of the natural qualities of his youth.

By this time, New York was his real home and the base of all his artistic activities. The Metropolitan had depended on him for many years, but with the war and the consequent problem of getting European artists to America, his presence was absolutely essential to the company's success. Caruso, too, just as badly needed the Metropolitan as the only remaining showcase for his talents.

The relationship between the New York opera company and its reigning star continued to be an excellent one, based on a rare degree of mutual loyalty and trust.

CARUSO SANG THE ROLE of the Duke in Rigoletto *at his début performances in London, New York, and Vienna. It was one of his most popular roles, and his recording of* La donna é mobile *remains one of his most popular recordings.*

So great was the trust in his later years that the tenor often performed without a formal contract. In business as well as in artistic matters, Otto Kahn and the board of directors of the Metropolitan had good reason to appreciate Caruso, who proved in every way to be an extraordinary gentleman. Though he often charged enormous fees away from the Metropolitan, the tenor never took advantage of the New York company's obvious dependence on him. Until the 1914–15 season, he had been paid $2,000 for each performance at the Metropolitan. When the time came to renew the agreement, it was assumed that he would ask for a huge increase; he was told that any figure up to $4,000 would be acceptable. Instead of demanding this large sum, or even more, Caruso told Kahn that he would be happy to settle for $2,500 and that anything above that would be too great a burden for him, with which he would not feel comfortable.

Even at that figure, which was considerably lower than that which he might have commanded, Caruso was the world's highest-paid opera singer. Yet, as was often repeated, he was always a bargain: an appearance by Caruso meant a sold-out house. His demands might have extended into other areas, such as choice of repertory, for during the years he sang in New York the repertory of the Metropolitan was dictated by his drawing power, yet, as a serious, intelligent artist, he chose only those operas which he felt were suitable for himself and for the company.

Sometimes, of course, both the Metropolitan and Caruso showed poor judgement in selecting a vehicle for the tenor. Such was the case with Bizet's *The Pearl Fishers*, which was performed on the night of 13 November 1916, shortly after Caruso's return to New York following his quiet summer in Italy. It was the opening night of the season, and he was eager to repeat one of his early successes for a new public — he had last sung it in Genoa with his close friend, the Roman baritone Giuseppe De Luca, in 1898, when the latter was only twenty-two years old. 'I feel as young as I did eighteen years ago,' he told a reporter. Unfortunately, neither the critics nor the public found much to praise in what one critic called 'Caruso's little Ceylon tea party', and the opera was withdrawn after three performances.

For the rest of the season, Caruso more than satisfied his public with his old favourites. As had become customary, his final appearance of the season — in *Rigoletto*,

OTTO KAHN, the brilliant chairman of the board of directors of the Metropolitan, was Caruso's friend and loyal supporter. Warm and unassuming in spite of his wealth, he showed his affection for the tenor by studying Italian so that he might better communicate with the company's star.

one of those old favourites, on 20 April 1917 — was an occasion for near hysteria. As the curtain came down on the end of the opera, the crowd simply refused to leave the theatre. Caruso bowed, he blew kisses and he waved his handkerchief at the audience. Finally, he found a new way to dismiss his fans, leading them in a rousing 'Three cheers for the United States', followed by 'Three cheers for the Allies'.

This farewell reflected the spirit of the times, and the year 1917 marked Caruso's emergence as a patriot. He played the role with boundless energy and dedication, giving his time and talent unselfishly by agreeing to any reasonable request to aid the cause of the Allies, by his participation in a concert or his presence at a bazaar. His older son, Rodolfo, had joined the Italian army; his younger son Enrico Jr was in Italy with his governess. After the entry of the United States into the war on 6

April 1917 his two countries were united in a common cause, which he enthusiastically supported. He felt it his duty to show his loyalty to both Italy (he was undeniably Italian and never gave up his citizenship) and the United States, a country he had learned to love and in which he had spent much of his life.

At the end of the long New York season, Caruso again set out on the Metropolitan's annual tour of what he sometimes called his 'step-mother' country. The highlight was his stay in Atlanta, his favourite of all American cities visited on the tour. His visits there were always a cause for celebration, and he joined in the spirit, bringing glamour and excitement to the city and delighting its citizens both on and off the stage. After his farewell performance in Atlanta where he sang three times in six days, he embarked on a more daring adventure, his first concert tour since 1908. Caruso enjoyed the opera tours with the Metropolitan, but concert tours were a different matter. He was a man of the theatre and did not enjoy singing before an audience, alone, without his costumes or his operatic props. In addition, he dreaded travelling to new places where he might run the risk of illness. Colds, sore throats and laryngitis were his constant enemies, and he felt immeasurably more secure and protected in New York, or at least in a major European city, than he did in less sophisticated surroundings.

In spite of this, in the early spring of 1917, F.C. Coppicus of the Metropolitan Musical Bureau persuaded him to take to the road once again for a limited tour of three cities — Cincinnati, Toledo and Pittsburgh — hoping that this short tour might convince the tenor to contemplate a more extensive tour in the future. These tours were enormously profitable to all concerned. Working with Coppicus was Edward L. Bernays, who was to serve as Caruso's press agent. Bernays, who enjoyed being called both 'the Caruso of press agents' and 'Caruso's press agent', never forgot the experience. In his memoirs, he wrote of the tenor:

> His glamour affected me as it did others. I was talking to the sun god, and the sun god by his light obliterated his surroundings. When we walked down Broadway together people forgot themselves and their interests for the moment and focused their attention on him . . . I recognized that I was letting the public's reaction to

Caruso affect my own attitudes. This is how people feel towards movie stars. I suppose identifying with someone who has achieved an extraordinary reputation is natural.

No film star could have been treated more grandly or greeted with more awe than was Caruso during that tour. 'Cincinnati basked in the radiant presence of Caruso,' wrote Bernays. And the tenor warmed to the town just as the town fell under his spell. He was followed by crowds wherever he went — in and out of shops and up and down the city's main streets. 'I felt as though I were walking on the boulevards of Paris with a popular monarch at the height of his glory,' Bernays wrote.

Caruso's charm and good humour temporarily disappeared, however, the evening before his concert, when a wedding party in a nearby room, complete with small orchestra, prevented him from getting the sleep he required. He was furious and demanded that the wedding party, and not he, be relocated. An embarrassed hotel manager told the revellers of the tenor's complaints, and the group good-naturedly agreed to move elsewhere in the hotel. After a night's rest, however, Caruso regained his good humour and sent the newly-weds an autographed photograph; on it, he wrote: 'Thank you for my *not* sleepless night.'

That evening, 4,000 people filled Cincinnati's Music Hall to listen to Caruso's first solo concert with orchestra and fortunately his lack of sleep did not appear to affect his performance. After the formal part of the programme, the applause was so prolonged that he was forced to sing twelve encores. 'Cincinnati surrendered to Caruso Tuesday night,' one local newspaper, the *Commercial Tribune* proclaimed the next day.

The next stop on the tour was Toledo, where another ecstatic welcome awaited the star. The setting for the concert in the industrial city was an unusual one. The Terminal Auditorium, a long narrow hall with more than a hundred rows of seats on an unraked floor, had formerly been a railway station, and it still resembled one. The audience, too, was unusual — more than 5,000 people, natives of the city as well as many hundreds of Italian-Americans brought there by special trains from Detroit and Sandusky, filled the hall. It was an audience as unsophisticated as was the setting.

It was a peculiar experience for the tenor, who was accustomed to the world's most elegant opera houses and audiences, though it was far less disturbing to him than was an episode which nearly spoilt his post-concert dinner at the Hotel Secor, when a waiter, unaware of the guest of honour's fear of a draught, opened a window to let some air into the overcrowded dining room. Reacting instinctively to the first trace of a breeze, Caruso, as unobtrusively as possible, placed himself under a table and away from the menacing draught, only returning to his chair when the window had been closed. He was grateful for the enthusiastic reception accorded him by the people of Toledo, but he did not want to catch a cold in their city.

A similar fear almost ruined Caruso's visit to Pittsburgh, the final stop of his tour, where he astonished his hosts by complaining on arrival that the bedroom of his luxurious suite at the Hotel Shenley, the best the city had to offer, was completely unsatisfactory. Everything, apparently, was wrong with it. He had been given a three-quarters bed, and he wanted a double bed. He had been provided with one mattress and two pillows, while he required no fewer than three mattresses and eighteen pillows. While the hotel staff frantically ransacked the premises in an effort to comply with the celebrity's outrageous demands, Caruso fulminated against the rigours of living in hotels in the American provinces, regaining his composure only after the extra pillows and mattresses had been located and brought to his room, enabling him to sleep high above the floor, in a nest of pillows which would protect him from the perils of a draught. It had been an unusual public display of temperament from a man eager to maintain the image of a good-natured entertainer, yet, in his own eyes, he had not been unduly wilful or demanding. His fear of catching a cold was an almost obsessive one, and he was merely exercising his right to do everything possible to protect his treasured voice.

The 3,400 people who packed Pittsburgh's new Shriner's Mosque the following evening would have agreed that Caruso should be allowed to do whatever he could to protect that voice. The tenor's concert, similar to those given in Cincinnati and Toledo, was an enormous success, further proof that, though still ill at ease without his costumes and props, he could triumph on the concert stage as he had in the opera house. The tour, with all its inconveniences, had been more gratifying than the tenor had anticipated. He took an almost boyish delight in the ingenuous warmth and good will which surrounded him at each stop. He had been accustomed to cheering crowds and to thunderous ovations, but the noisy bands that met his train, the flags waved vigorously at his appearances and the unsophisticated speeches of welcome represented a refreshing change from the more formal and more worldly receptions of the past. Furthermore, and this could not help but please him, the tour was an enormous success financially. Although his performances were relatively short, the fee he received for each concert was almost double what he had been paid for singing at the Metropolitan.

CARUSO'S FAME SPREAD through his many recordings — he made almost five hundred of them — issued by Pathé, Zonophone, the Gramophone Company, and the Victor Talking Machine Company. He signed a contract with the latter in 1909, giving the company the exclusive right to make and sell records of his voice for the entire world for a period of twenty-five years.

17

A COMPLETE ARTIST

Only five days after his Pittsburgh concert, Caruso, having been forced to abandon his annual summer holiday in Italy because of the hazards of travel in wartime Europe, and having accepted an unprecedented offer of $200,000 for a total of thirty performances, set out on another tour of South America. He had been reluctant to accept the offer because of his fear of meeting Ada Giachetti who was living in Buenos Aires. During his last visit, their paths had not crossed, but this time the tenor felt certain that they would meet, and he badly wanted to avoid an unpleasant encounter. He need not have feared such a meeting. The two did see each other on several occasions, and their encounters were extremely warm, lending credence to the belief of Caruso's friends that he and Ada, who kept up a more than friendly correspondence, were in love until the tenor's death.

From the day of his arrival, even before his first performance, the South American tour was a tiring one. For the three weeks before the official opening of the season in Buenos Aires, Caruso was on display in Saō Paulo, Rio, and Santos, the centre of attention wherever he travelled, greeted with curiosity by the press and lavishly entertained by his Brazilian admirers. He was followed through the streets, fêted at official banquets, and the prime attraction at benefits, even when not performing. No effort was spared by the management of the tour in its attempts to stimulate sales in order to recover the huge investment that had been made to bring the world's greatest tenor back to South America.

A MATURE, SERIOUS CARUSO in a photograph taken in 1917.

The tour itself was not without its problems. In fact, once Caruso began to sing, his performances were so overwhelmed by the accompanying publicity that they often proved anticlimactic, and the reaction to them was frequently disappointing. This time the tenor was competing again not only with the Caruso of the past but also with a legend overzealously cultivated by the press and the publicity machine that relentlessly fed it. The reaction to this ballyhoo was inevitable, and it was often reflected in the negative reviews by critics who had previously praised the tenor and by audiences who, tired of the fanfare and angered by the high prices, did not hesitate to show their disappointment on quite a number of occasions.

The tour was also marred by petty jealousies and misunderstandings, but, on balance, it was a successful one, from which both Caruso and the management profited handsomely. Even audiences who had been prepared to express disapproval, in the end found themselves cheering, and the tenor's popularity was so great that his scheduled thirty appearances increased to forty.

Caruso arrived in New York in the autumn of 1917 accompanied by cases of gold which he had received in payment for his South American appearances. The golden-voiced tenor, one reporter quipped, had, appropriately, been paid in gold. Once again, in spite of enormous difficulties, the Metropolitan had managed to bring an impressive array of singers to New York, among them John McCormack, singing for the first time as a regular member of the company.

Both tenors were assets to the company, but Caruso's presence was more important than ever, since all German operas (with the exception of *Martha*, presumably because it was sung in Italian) had been banned for the duration of the war, and the Italian and French operas Caruso sang completely dominated the season's repertory. From his opening-night performance in *Aida* to his farewell in *L'Elisir d'Amore* on 19 April 1918, Caruso sang twelve different roles. A few critics complained that his voice showed signs of strain, and others noted a deterioration in his breath control, but most who heard him agreed with James Huneker, who, after a performance of *Pagliacci*, wrote that 'his voice is now at its richest, his acting is more polished every performance'. In the course of the season, the tenor sang three roles he had never sung before in New York, and two of these must be numbered among his few failures. One was that of Flamen in Mascagni's *Lodoletta* — he was far more highly praised than was the opera — and the other was the role of Avito in a far more effective opera, Italo Montemezzi's *L'Amore dei Tre Re*, a role which afforded him little opportunity to display his talent and which he dropped from his repertoire following his three performances that season.

Caruso's performance of his third new role, that of John of Leyden in Meyerbeer's *Le Prophète*, which he sang on 7 February 1918, more than made up for these two disappointments. Once more, as with Samson a few years before, he was facing the challenge of a role meant for a dramatic tenor — his good friend Chaliapin had even warned him against singing it for fear that it might ruin his voice. In spite of this warning, Caruso, guided by a sure knowledge of what he could and could not do, as well as an awareness of the direction his artistic career must follow in his mature years — he was approaching his forty-fifth birthday — took up the challenge.

His first performance in *Le Prophète* confirmed his instinctive judgement; the opera provided him with one of the most solid triumphs of his career. Critics agreed unanimously that he was not merely the possessor of a great voice, but that he had become a complete artist.

The war made it impossible for Caruso to travel to Europe in the summer of 1918. Instead, in spite of tempting offers from South America, he decided to spend the summer in the United States, keeping himself busy as best he could.

He continued his efforts in support of the Allied cause, and his frequent appearances as a fund-raiser, marked by his customary energy and charm, were enormously successful. In addition to these benefits, Caruso gave two concerts of his own. The first was at the seaside resort of Ocean Grove, New Jersey, where a crowd of 12,000 people packed into an auditorium with space for 10,000 to cheer their idol, who especially delighted them with his rousing interpretation of George M. Cohan's 'Over There'. The second was at the fashionable spa of Saratoga Springs, New York, where both he and his friend Scotti were on holiday.

This holiday was well deserved, for during the summer Caruso had also been at work on his first, and last, films. The motion picture industry was flourishing, and to one

SCOTTI in a drawing by Caruso. Born in Naples in 1866, he first met Caruso in 1898 and remained the tenor's close friend and colleague until the latter's death.

enterprising producer, Jesse L. Lasky, it seemed only logical that cinemas could be filled with audiences who wanted to see the world's favourite tenor, even if they could not hear him. It had worked with Geraldine Farrar, who had become a star of the silent screen, so why not Caruso, who was loved not only for his voice but also for his undeniable charisma and common touch? Caruso was offered more than $200,000 for approximately six weeks' work — the producer decided to make two films rather than one during this period, thereby halving the risk.

From Caruso's point of view, it was a new and potentially profitable challenge, as well as an opportunity to be seen by millions who would never have a chance to watch him in person. It would also stimulate the sales of his records all over the country, to the satisfaction of the Victor Company which eagerly agreed to help in the promotion of the films.

Caruso took his work seriously and maintained a gruelling pace throughout the production of the films. He arose early, taking his morning coffee at six, and inevitably arrived at the studio, a former riding academy in New York, ahead of schedule. His director, Edward José, was both surprised and impressed by his new star's conscientiousness. Furthermore, Caruso's good humour never flagged, despite the enervating heat. There were no displays of temperament, from the first day to the last. As always, in spite of his practical jokes, which he practised on the set as he did on the stage, Caruso was a professional, even in a field completely new to him.

Unfortunately, his seriousness was not rewarded; for once the Caruso magic failed completely. The first film was called *My Cousin*, and in it the star assumed two roles, that of a great tenor and that of his cousin, an impoverished artist, whose success as a lover depended on the credibility of his relationship to the tenor. When the film opened, it was so poorly received that the second film, to be called *The Great Romance* or *The Splendid Romance*, in which the tenor played the role of a pianist-prince, was withdrawn before its first public screening. Obviously the public was not interested in a voiceless Caruso. 'Candidly, if you cannot hear his marvellous tenor voice,' the reviewer for *Photoplay Journal* wrote, 'you cannot possibly enjoy Caruso much . . . You cannot help but wish the star would step through the silversheet and offer just one tiny song.'

18
HABITS,
HOBBIES
and a
BRIDE

Often during his career Caruso was asked how he spent his time away from the stage; his reply was always the same: 'I work.' This simple answer was accurate, and while he worked the tenor insisted on maintaining a rigorous schedule, which allowed for little variation in his daily routine.

In New York a typical day for Caruso began at eight in the morning when he was awakened by his valet. A bath followed, one of at least two that he took each day. Fastidious since childhood, he was inordinately concerned with personal hygiene and grooming. He splashed himself with perfume and used to walk around his apartment with an atomizer, spraying each room with scent.

Following his bath, he turned his attention to his throat, treating it with gargles and sprays that were applied at regular intervals throughout the day. A rubdown and often a visit by a barber followed: his external appearance, Caruso felt, reflected his inner well-being. After dressing, his clothes having been carefully selected and laid out by one of his valets, it was time for a light breakfast of black coffee and dry toast, after which the tenor was ready to receive an occasional visitor.

By ten o'clock, and this was a firm rule, it was time to begin his work. If no rehearsal was scheduled, this meant a session with his accompanist, exercising his voice and preparing roles he would be singing within the next few days. If, instead, the tenor was to rehearse at the Metro-politan, he would walk the short distance from his home at the Knickerbocker Hotel to the theatre, inevitably arriving there on time — punctuality was another of his obsessions.

His behaviour during rehearsals was exemplary, and he also seemed to believe that it was his personal responsibil-ity to make the often tiring sessions as pleasant as possible, joking with and encouraging his colleagues, though never failing to pay close attention to the conductor and the stage director. There were no unreasonable outbursts of temper, nor did the tenor ever balk at going over and over the material to get it right, no matter how tedious.

Following rehearsals, Caruso would go to lunch, usu-ally at a small neighbourhood restaurant. His meal would be a simple one: lamb chops or the white meat of chicken and spinach were his favourites. After this spartan lunch — reports of the robust tenor, who weighed at least 180 lbs and was slightly more than 5 ft 8 ins tall, hungrily devouring huge plates of spaghetti might occasionally have been accurate, but only during his rare holidays and never, in his mature years, during the opera season — he returned to his hotel. There he took care of his correspondence and again saw visitors until it was time for an early dinner, a simple meal, consisting most often of a minute steak, vegetables and ice cream.

His was the life of an athlete in training for several months during the year, but his routine was even more severe on those days preceding an evening performance at the opera house. Lunch was then his final meal until after the performance. With the exception of two apples, one preceding the opera and one between the acts, he would eat nothing until a light supper at midnight. After his lunch, he would return to his apartment to prepare himself, emotionally and physically, for his night's work.

The pre-performance dressing-room ritual, from the time of his arrival at the opera house a few hours before curtain time until his first entrance on the stage, was often described by journalists privileged to watch him, but no account is more amusing than that in New York's *Evening Post* of 31 January 1914 which read, in part:

> Caruso sits before a stationary washstand and one of the valets hands him a toothbrush and powder. Then for three solid minutes by his Swiss-movement watch does Caruso cleanse and scrub and polish. The ever alert dressers stand behind him, watchful for a shrug of

his shoulders, which they immediately interpret into a command. Caruso takes a long breath — and he needs it. It must be a signal, for one of the valets has a glass of warm water in one hand and in the other a big, round, pasteboard box full of little brownish crystals. Caruso takes a handful of the crystals and drops them into the warm water, where they dissolve immediately.

'That's gargling salt,' he says. 'I use it for my first gargle.' The gargle takes four minutes and then comes the vaporizer. A glass of water containing bicarbonate of soda and glycerine is placed in a little stand; a rubber hose connected with the vaporizer is put into the glass, and a thin, forceful sputtering spray shoots out a full foot. Into this tiny Gatling-gun spray Caruso plunges, mouth open.

Then the heavy artillery answers the little Gatling gun — for Caruso coughs back at the spray, chokes, bellows and sputters. Into each nostril, then deep into the throat, go the bicarbonate of soda and glycerine over and over and over again, until Caruso coughs no more. 'Now it is clear,' he says and rises. 'You have no idea how much dirt can collect in the throat and nose in one day's time.'

The vaporizer bath has taken eight minutes by Caruso's infallible watch; but the end is not yet. There is a cold water gargle — sterilized water, please — minus the salt, to follow; and that, in turn, by a spray for the nose only, of a very dark colour, the name of which Caruso could not recall. Only about six sniffs a piece for each nostril and the spray is put away.

Then menthol and Vaseline on absorbent cotton are attached to long sticks and Caruso swabs out his throat with these as a gunner would a cannon. 'Dilates the throat,' he says between gasps. One more gargle of cold water and the homage to the throat is finished.

It has taken twenty-two minutes!

On goes his bathrobe and he is in the corridor — smoking a cigarette! Twenty-two minutes of hard work he had given to that throat — and now he is calmly smoking a cigarette and inhaling every blessed puff of it! Shades of bicarbonate of soda, of gargling salt and glycerine and of menthol — and of what avail are you when a nervous man wants a cigarette – and wants it now?

Once the throat treatment had been concluded, make-up was applied, with Caruso carefully keeping his eyes and mouth closed to avoid potentially damaging powder — after which, he lit another cigarette. Finally, it was time for the two valets to dress the star.

Outwardly prepared for the performance, Caruso then began to exercise his voice. No matter how perfectly he was dressed and made up — and he was unfailingly meticulous about each detail — it was his voice that mattered most. Full of nervous energy, he paced up and down the corridor, exchanging occasional banter with his fellow performers, retiring to his room to spend some of that energy on his caricatures, emerging again from time to time for another walk in the corridor, another cigarette . . . No matter how often he had sung a role, each new appearance was preceded by an often terrifying attack of nerves. Caruso commented:

> Every man who gives of his best must be very watchful that he gives it. That makes him conscious of himself — then he becomes nervous; fearful that he may not give full measure. Stage fright is the price one pays for being an artist.

The tension that had been built up, and then released on stage, accounted in part for the excitement that was communicated to the audience in the course of a Caruso performance. More than a glorious voice, his was a vibrating presence. This tremendous expenditure of energy, inevitably, took its toll. It was reported that the tenor lost an average of three pounds each time he sang; he himself admitted that he was exhausted at the end of an evening's work, although the feeling of tiredness did not overcome him until a quarter of an hour after the performance, when he was finally able to relax, greet the admirers who waited for him at the Metropolitan's stage door, and leave for a light midnight supper, usually no more than cold chicken, consommé and toast.

During the Metropolitan season, Caruso averaged two performances a week, a schedule which severely limited his outside activities; but there were apparently few, if any, of these that he missed. When not singing, his evenings were usually spent quietly. He rarely went to the theatre or to concerts and attended performances of the opera only when especially interested in the work of

one of his colleagues. Parties bored him and he was ill at ease at them. He preferred to remain in his apartment, quietly organizing his scrapbooks (collections of his press clippings as well as First World War cartoons), arranging his growing stamp collection, and working on his caricatures, which were a great source of satisfaction to him, and through which he revealed a remarkably sensitive eye, a genuine talent for draftsmanship, and a keen and gentle sense of humour.

Though surrounded by servants, sycophants and admirers, he had few intimate friends — Scotti, Calvin Child, Victor's director of artists and repertoire, and, during his later years, Bruno Zirato, his first official secretary and later the manager of the New York Philharmonic, among them. As for women friends, the press had for several years been silent about the tenor's romances; journalists presumably were unaware of his lengthy relationship with Rina Giachetti, Ada's sister. Because of this, the announcement on 21 August 1918 that the previous day Caruso had married Miss Dorothy Park Benjamin came as a shock — to his friends, his associates, his fans, and, especially, to Rina Giachetti. Obviously referring to the latter, Puccini wrote to Sybil Seligman upon hearing of the marriage: 'Heaven knows how badly it will affect "X"; she has been behaving in Italy as though she were the wife of the great tenor and the guardian of his son.'

Caruso's choice of bride was even more surprising than the fact of his unexpected marriage. Dorothy Benjamin, twenty years younger than he, was a tall, blonde, broad-shouldered young woman with a pleasant face that showed, unmistakably, all the signs of good breeding. The child of a socially prominent family, her background was diametrically opposed to that of Caruso. Perhaps it was just that disparity of background that appealed most to the tenor. He had gained both fame and fortune, and these had enabled him to live a life of luxury and acquire a magnificent villa in Tuscany, thereby distancing himself from the streets of Naples. But, in the eyes of many, he remained merely an entertainer — albeit an enormously successful one — of humble origins. By marrying Dorothy, he might have felt that he could gain the social status otherwise denied him.

In spite of her wealth, Dorothy's childhood and adolescence had not been happy. Her father, Park Benjamin, was an authority on naval affairs and the author of a

CARUSO

celebrated book on electricity, and the Benjamin home in New York was frequented by the leading intellectuals of the time. Her mother was taken ill when Dorothy was eleven years old, and, as a result, the girl was sent away to the Convent of the Sacred Heart near Philadelphia at the age of thirteen. Four years later, she was summoned home to take care of her father.

Life in the joyless household was impossible for the young girl. Her father was ill-tempered and domineering; he made no effort to conceal his contempt for his daughter, criticizing her appearance, reminding her of what he considered to be her ignorance, and refusing to allow her friends to come to the house. After a year, bored with his daughter, he convinced a thirty-year-old Italian, Anna Bolchi, to live with him, to act as a companion to Dorothy and to take charge of the household.

Miss Bolchi filled her role admirably, though she proved to be a better companion to Park Benjamin than to his shy and lonely daughter. They shared a love of music, and she accompanied him to the opera, and entertained him with her own singing. With her arrival, the house came to life; friends were invited to dinner, and Miss Bolchi played the role of the charming hostess.

Though Dorothy was excluded from these activities, she had good reason to be grateful to Miss Bolchi, for it was through her, several years later, that she met Enrico Caruso. According to Dorothy's memoirs, from the moment she first saw him at a christening party, she knew they would marry. Their courtship, if it can be called that, was a brief one. Miss Bolchi invited Caruso to the Benjamin home for dinner, and he soon became a frequent visitor, presumably enjoying the company of his host and hostess and often reciprocating by sending them tickets for the opera. Dorothy, who was apparently ignored during their dinners together, was nonetheless included in these invitations to the opera.

Three months after their first evening together, Dorothy had her first meeting alone with Caruso. He was going home after a visit to Park Benjamin, and offered to drop the young woman off at the home of a friend, with whom she was having dinner. During the drive, he proposed marriage and she accepted. A few months later, they were married — without the blessings of Park Benjamin, who never forgave the couple and never saw his daughter again.

19

AFTER *the* WAR: *a* SUMMER *at* BELLOSGUARDO *and* OTHER ADVENTURES

There was no honeymoon for the newly-weds — 'We intend to make every day a honeymoon,' the bride informed reporters. Instead, Caruso energetically resumed his rounds of fundraising concerts, this time singing before audiences not only eager to see and hear him, but also curious to get a look at the new Mrs Caruso. New Yorkers, in search of romance, took the couple to their hearts and cheered their every public appearance, even if some wondered why the celebrated tenor had chosen a shy, unglamorous young American to be his bride.

Dorothy's first official public appearance took place on 31 August 1918, when her husband sang at Speedway Park, Sheepshead Bay, Brooklyn. The occasion was the New York City Police Department's Field Day. McCormack and Amato were among the performers, but all eyes were on the newly-weds. Caruso was patriotically dressed in a royal blue coat, with a flaming red tie and white flannel trousers. He was given a police escort for the ride to Brooklyn and was loudly cheered by the throng of 125,000 people as he entered the field, his young bride at his side.

Though the war was approaching its end, the mood of the country remained patriotic, and throughout the month of September the tenor continued to perform at benefits to aid the war effort. His last such appearance, before resuming his professional commitments, took place on the night of 30 September when he joined McCormack,

THE TENOR AT SPEEDWAY PARK, *Sheepshead Bay, Brooklyn, on 31 August 1918, where 125,000 people joined him in singing 'Over There'. In the course of the afternoon's festivities, almost $300,000 was raised to purchase equipment for the New York police reserves; as a result, the tenor was appointed an officer in those reserves. Four months later, when he was presented with his official badge, he asked if he was entitled to make arrests. When told that he was, he suggested he might go right to the Metropolitan and make an arrest or two!*

Galli-Curci, and the seventeen-year-old violin prodigy Jascha Heifetz in a Liberty Loan concert at Carnegie Hall. Following this, he and his wife left for what was to be the start of another extended concert tour. This time, his fears of infection in the American hinterlands were justified, for they arrived in Buffalo, the first stop of the tour, during an influenza epidemic of such proportions that local authorities forced a cancellation of the concert, in the belief that a large gathering would constitute a menace to the health of the city. Caruso was grateful to be relieved of his commitment, but before leaving the city he good-naturedly agreed to sing informally at a concert at a local hotel. His patriotism was rewarded — nearly a million dollars' worth of Liberty Bonds were sold there — but his worst fears were almost realized when, while eating at the hotel, a fellow diner sneezed in the direction of the honoured guests. Terrified, Caruso, leading his wife by the hand, immediately returned to his suite, where he vigorously sprayed his nose and throat, inhaled vapours, and did what else he could to disinfect himself. It was

CARUSO

a disturbing experience, and, with the exception of one short stop in Detroit, where the tenor was assured there was no possibility of infection, the tour was cancelled.

Untouched by the germs he had so profoundly feared, Caruso returned to New York to prepare for the opening of the Metropolitan which was triumphant in every way; it took place on the night of 11 November 1918, the night all America was celebrating the armistice that brought an end to the First World War. The opera was *Samson et Dalila*, and the gala performance provided a rousing climax to a day of jubilation. The mood in the opera house was festive, and, following the first act, the curtain was raised, revealing the entire company, gathered together to stage an impromptu 'victory pageant'. Caruso, still dressed as Samson, held a large Italian flag; Louise Homer, the Delilah, waved an American flag; and other members of the company proudly unfurled the flags of the other Allied nations. The performance of the opera, too, was superb, with Caruso singing at his best. Henry E. Krehbiel of the *New York Tribune* wrote:

> There has only been one Samson in the Metropolitan Opera House, and it is a woeful reflection of what may befall Saint-Saëns' opera, and even the institution itself, when in the course of time Signor Caruso shall bear away with himself the pillars upon which the house stand. Fortunately, there was nothing in last night's representation to indicate that such a catastrophe is immediately impending.

Throughout the season, Caruso sang ten different roles, again revealing a more mature presence dramatically as well as vocally. Musically, the most important performance that season took place on 15 November, when he sang the role of Alvaro in Verdi's *La Forza del Destino* for the first time (it was also the opera's first performance at the Metropolitan). The tenor was at his best — his singing was 'glorious' according to James Huneker. But even more notable and surprising on that occasion was the brilliant début of a young soprano, Rosa Ponselle — later to become one of the great singers of her time — who might not have been there had it not been for Caruso's help. The daughter of immigrant Neapolitan parents, she was born Rosa Ponzillo in Meridan, Connecticut in 1897. Part of a vaudeville act with her sister Carmela, which had

achieved a moderate success at a number of small theatres, the young woman came to the attention of Caruso, who first heard her sing at her teacher's studio. She impressed Caruso who enthusiastically recommended her to Gatti-Casazza, who was looking for a soprano to sing the role of Leonore in Verdi's opera. Gatti auditioned both sisters for the role, but he hired only Rosa, even though the frightened young woman had fainted in the middle of the audition.

His judgement was sound, and Rosa Ponselle's story is an extraordinary one. Only six months after Caruso had first heard her sing, the totally inexperienced soprano — she had only *been* to the opera twice, once to hear Caruso and Farrar in *Madama Butterfly* — was singing opposite the great tenor on the stage of the Metropolitan.

Though the musical highlight of the Metropolitan's season was that performance of *La Forza del Destino*, an event of greater sentimental importance took place on the night of 22 March 1919. It was a gala performance celebrating the twenty-fifth year of Caruso's career, a chance for the company to pay tribute to the man who had dominated it for fifteen years. Caruso had been embarrassed by the elaborate preparations for this gala evening in his honour and agreed to the celebration only on the condition that the proceeds were donated to the Emergency Fund, to benefit the company's musicians. The evening was one of the most festive and glamorous in the opera house's history. Caruso sang one act of each of three operas and received gifts and tributes from all over the world. He was greatly moved by what was described in New York's *Morning Telegraph* as 'the most memorable, the most spontaneous, and the most affectionate demonstration of personal and artistic admiration that New York has ever bestowed on any man or woman.'

Though praised as a national American hero, Caruso was eager to return to his own home at the Villa Bellosguardo, which he had not seen for two years. He missed his two sons, and he was anxious to show his magnificent villa to Dorothy, whom he wanted to introduce to his children and to his Italian family and friends.

His first opportunity to travel there came in the summer of 1919, following the usual post-season Metropolitan tour. That summer, however, was not nearly as idyllic as he had anticipated. Dorothy had difficulty adjusting. Though enchanted by the villa and its gardens, she was

less than comfortable with her introduction to Italian family life and to her husband's enormous entourage, which filled the villa throughout their stay there. As she later wrote, she was often lonely though never alone.

Her relationship with her husband's sons was difficult. Mimmi needed more warmth and affection than she could give him, and any communication with Fofò, barely twenty-one-years old, was impossible, since the young man spoke no English and Dorothy no Italian. There was also a language barrier between Dorothy and the many other relatives (including Caruso's brother Giovanni and his stepmother) and friends who populated the villa — in her memoirs Dorothy admitted she was never quite sure who most of them were.

For his part, Caruso involved himself as little as possible in the problems and conflicts of the household. He kept busy working; an accompanist came from Florence to work with him each morning, going over the score of Halévy's *La Juive*, which he was to sing in the autumn, while Dorothy, left alone, busied herself by redecorating parts of the villa and working in the flower garden.

The summer ended on a particularly bitter note, which had nothing to do with the linguistic and social conflicts within the villa. Post-war Italy was in a state of chaos, and social discontent threatened to lead to open revolution. The Carusos, living in isolation in their splendid villa, were a natural target for the anger of the poor, and one morning Bellosguardo was invaded by a group of more than a hundred women and children who complained to the gatekeeper that they were hungry and demanded to see the world-famous singer. Caruso agreed to see them, listened sympathetically to their complaints, and ordered an enormous picnic to be prepared for the hungry mob. This, he believed, was the only way he could satisfy them.

They, however, were not so easily satisfied, for within a short time five trucks carrying some 150 men waving red flags drove up to the gates of the villa. Smashing their way through the gates, they reached Caruso and angrily informed him that they had come to hang his caretaker and confiscate the huge amount of food stored in the villa. The tenor was livid; if they wanted to hang anyone, they would have to hang him, he told them. When they calmed down he turned over his supplies of wheat, wine and oil, asking only that they leave enough food for him and his family until they left the villa for America.

CARUSO

THE TENOR *seems somewhat uncomfortable standing between two Mexican women during his month-long season in Mexico City in the autumn of 1919.*

It had been a terrifying experience. Fofò, in the uniform of the Italian army, had wisely remained in hiding during the raid. Dorothy, according to Mimmi, was 'scared skinny'. And Caruso was hurt, stunned that his initial act of generosity had not pacified the angry mob and, finally, horrified when he learned that most of the food had been thrown away in the middle of the town square immediately after the raid.

It was with great relief that the Carusos arrived in New York on 3 September; with them was young Mimmi, whom they felt would benefit from an American education. (He was sent to boarding school, first in Connecticut and then in Indiana.) They had little time to spend together, however, since only a few weeks after their

154

arrival, Caruso embarked on his first tour of Mexico which had been arranged the previous February. This meant a month-long separation, as it was considered best for Dorothy, six months pregnant at the time, not to accompany her husband on his foreign travels.

It was a separation that pained both of them, but it was unavoidable. Their first year together had not been the endless honeymoon Dorothy had foreseen. As a husband, Caruso had proved to be jealous, possessive and demanding, just as he had also been unfailingly generous and affectionate. He had never hidden the fact that his work came first, no matter how it affected his personal life. Furthermore, this Mexican trip was a financial necessity. Caruso's earnings were tremendous, but so were his expenses. He was as generous with others as he was with himself. His youngest son estimated that there were as many as 250 people on his father's unofficial payroll. They included Ada Giachetti, members of his family in Naples, old friends who had helped him in the past, and countless penniless opera singers all over the world. Because of this, though the money came in regularly, it went out just as regularly, and earnings from a tour in a foreign country — not taxable in the United States — were essential, just to enable him to pay his American taxes.

Unfortunately, Caruso's Mexican season was far from an unqualified success. He was, once again, troubled by headaches and neck pains, and again faced those problems which had plagued him in the past: too much advance publicity, and too many comparisons with the youthful Caruso. In addition, the tenor's high fee, $7,000 a performance, once again made it impossible for the management to hire artists of major stature to appear with him and thereby ensure effective, balanced productions.

In all, Caruso sang twelve times during his month in Mexico. He sang at the Teatro Esperanza Iris, and he sang five times in El Toreo, an enormous bullfight arena which held more than 20,000 people, once during a heavy rainstorm. His physical suffering, his entire body was often wracked with pain, had been even greater than his discomfort at singing with artists who were at best mediocre. Nonetheless, he managed to win the hearts of the Mexican public, and after his final appearance he was able to telegraph to Dorothy: '25,000 people. Am happy have been here and knowing this country and enthusiastic people that gave me continually great sensations.'

20
TRIUMPH
and DECLINE

Less than two weeks after his troubled visit to Mexico, Caruso was grateful to be back at the Metropolitan, opening the season with his familiar colleagues Farrar and Scotti in a performance of *Tosca*. Apart from *Tosca*, which he sang only once, *Manon Lescaut, Pagliacci, L'Elisir d'Amore* and *Martha*, the tenor concentrated his efforts during the season on his heavier, more dramatic roles in *Samson et Dalila, La Forza del Destino*, and *Le Prophète*, and undertook one new role, that of Eléazar in *La Juive*, his thirty-seventh role at the opera house.

Caruso's appearance, on the afternoon of 22 November, as Eléazar, was, according to Irving Kolodin, historian of the Metropolitan, 'without doubt the most striking artistic triumph of his career'. More than ever, he revealed himself to be something more than merely a great singer — he was a consummate artist, able to bring to life every facet of a complex dramatic figure in a striking portrayal that brought him extraordinary acclaim, even for a man accustomed to great acclaim.

Caruso sensed the importance of the occasion. Unconsciously, he seems to have been preparing for the role of the humble Jewish goldsmith for many years; he had in the past, whenever possible, attended synagogue services so that he might study what he felt were the unique vocal methods of cantors in uniting words and music. During the previous summer in Italy, he had studied the new role with even more than his usual intensity. Back in

CARUSO'S LAST — and perhaps his greatest — triumph, in the role of the Jewish goldsmith, Eléazar, in Halévy's 1835 opera, La Juive. *With him is the young American soprano, Rosa Ponselle, who sang the role of Rachel when the opera was revived at the Metropolitan on the afternoon of 22 November 1919. It was Caruso who suggested to Gatti-Casazza that the young soprano be hired by the Metropolitan.*

157

New York he spent hours in the library, making sure that each detail of his characterization would be accurate, that his make-up and costumes would be in keeping with the requirements of the role.

His efforts were well rewarded, and the critics agreed that his performance, in a part that was both vocally and dramatically extraordinarily well suited to him, marked a milestone in his career. It was, wrote the reviewer for the *New York Tribune*, 'an interpretation which will remain long in the memory of those who saw it.'

It was in the role of Eléazar that Caruso concluded his seventeenth season at the Metropolitan on the night of 23 April 1920, before a cheering crowd that was, more than ever, reluctant to see him go. There was no extended American tour that year — Caruso had committed himself to only three performances in Atlanta — and after his previous experiences in Italy he was not eager to return to Europe; instead, he chose to set off on another tour of a Latin-American country, namely Cuba.

Once again, his wife had to be left behind, this time to take care of their infant daughter, Gloria, who had been born on 18 December 1919. Instead, Dorothy, the baby, members of Dorothy's family, and a huge staff of servants were sent to East Hampton, Long Island, where the tenor had rented 'The Creeks', an enormous estate belonging to Albert Herter, for the summer months — an estate which equalled in luxury his own villa in Tuscany. Set among a hundred acres on the shores of Georgica Lake, two miles from the village, it included, in addition to the main house, a guest house, a housekeeper's cottage, sumptuous gardens, fountains and a tennis court. None of the pleasures afforded by such a home could be enjoyed by Caruso, however, until he concluded his professional commitments at the end of June.

Caruso's motive for the tour, again, was money; this time he was to be paid the astounding (for the time) sum of $10,000 for each of ten evening performances and half that for each of two matinées. It is unlikely, however, that any sum of money would have compensated for the troubles he endured on a trip which was even less happy than his visit to Mexico had been. Painful headaches plagued him even more than they had in the past, and, in addition, he suffered from Havana's stifling heat which robbed him of his badly-needed sleep. For the first time in his life he had a toothache. In view of his often-expressed, if

medically unproven, belief that his teeth were a source of his strength, he felt this to be a particularly bad omen.

Equally serious, he was again faced with a problem beyond his control — the enormous pre-tour ballyhoo which this time was creating an ugly hostility he was unable to combat. Both press and public were outraged by the prices the impresario charged for each Caruso performance, and, well in advance of his first appearance, he was the subject of vicious attacks in the local press, most of which blamed these high prices on the extravagant fees demanded by Caruso. To make matters even worse, journalists warned of what they called his waning vocal powers and predicted a disastrous season.

In the course of his first two performances, in *Martha*, the initial coolness of the public was transformed into warm applause — the Caruso magic remained effective — but the press remained stubbornly hostile, comparing him unfavourably to other contemporary tenors. He was

THIS PHOTOGRAPH OF THE TENOR, his wife, and their daughter, Gloria, was taken at the Herter estate, in fashionable East Hampton, Long Island, which they rented for the summer of 1920.

CARUSO, who enjoyed clowning wherever he went, is shown here in Havana, cranking up the motor of the car. Though he enjoyed owning automobiles, he never learnt to drive.

indignant, and before his third appearance he wrote to Dorothy: 'Tomorrow we go with "Elisir", and if they will not be satisfay, I will go away from this hot place.' Happily, in spite of his continuing physical discomfort, the performance of Donizetti's opera was well received as were several later appearances. Nevertheless, certain members of the press continued to carp, complaining insistently of the high prices charged for what they considered to be inferior performances. Admittedly, the prices were high, and a certain resentment could be justified. The pianist Artur Rubinstein, in Havana at the time, explained in his memoirs that Caruso's fee for each performance 'represented years of work for an average inhabitant. It was no wonder that you could feel a certain hostility in the audience.'

That simmering hostility turned to open violence during Caruso's last appearance in Havana, when a forcible explosion shook the theatre during the second act of *Aida*. It was a frightening experience, described here by the impresario Adolfo Bracale:

> The bomb exploded with a roar. Instantly total confusion reigned with cries of terror as some of the decorative figures adorning the proscenium arch of the stage began to fall in shattered hunks. One of the balcony columns collapsed, injuring some of the audience, and in the pit the harp and the tympani were totally destroyed ... The supers fled into the street in their Egyptian costumes, while the choristers and dancers screamed like the martyrs of Zaragossa. Caruso, attired as Radames, was with me in my office when the bomb exploded and both of us hurried out on to the stage, dodging bits of scenery, to beg the audience to remain calm.

The tenor, still in the costume of the Egyptian warrior, was taken at once to his hotel where he recovered his composure. Nonetheless, the incident continued to haunt him, and bitterness towards the Cuban press, which he felt responsible for the incident, remained even after his return to the United States, when he wrote an angry letter to Havana's leading newspaper complaining of his treatment while in Cuba.

Equally disturbing to Caruso during his last days in Havana was word that Dorothy's jewellery, valued

at almost half a million dollars, had been stolen from the couple's summer home on Long Island. The tenor was shaken when the news was given to him by a representative of the Associated Press, but he was somewhat comforted by a cable from Dorothy assuring him that she and the baby were well and that everything possible was being done to apprehend the criminal. He replied with a cable of his own: 'Thanks God you and baby are safe. Will replace jewels.'

During the next twenty-four hours, further details of the robbery reached Havana. The story was certainly a frightening one. Dorothy and her sister-in-law had been in the library alone, when they heard the alarm in the bedroom safe, which contained all the jewellery, go off. They rushed upstairs, found that the safe had been removed, and that the bedroom window had been broken. After a frantic search by a number of servants, the safe — opened and emptied of its contents — was found on the lawn, not far from the house.

An intensive investigation, led by police and insurance detectives, began at once. Though it soon became obvious that the crime had been committed by someone familiar with the house, Dorothy insisted that it had not been an inside job. However, the possibility that the premises had been staked out in advance was not discarded.

When, a few weeks later — Caruso had committed himself to finishing his Cuban tour and making two appearances in the United States before returning to Long Island — the tenor arrived at the Herter estate, the atmosphere was still tense. Detectives swarmed about the house and grounds in the hope of uncovering clues that might lead to the identity of the thieves, endlessly interrogating the family and all the many servants. Dorothy, Gloria and Mimmi were under constant surveillance: a letter had been received from the Black Hand, threatening to kidnap both children.

Caruso was deeply distressed by this invasion of his privacy. He was disturbed too, because, since his return home, he had conducted informal investigations of his own which had convinced him that the robbery had been an inside job, in spite of Dorothy's denials. When, finally, the insurance company gave up its efforts to recover the jewellery and handed Caruso a cheque to compensate for the loss, he immediately tore it up. He wanted no further investigations, no intimations that he himself might be covering up for a member of his household.

A PUBLICITY PHOTOGRAPH *of Caruso, the greatest of recording stars.*

CARUSO

The matter, as far as he was concerned, was closed, and for the rest of the summer Caruso did his best to relax. It was not easy for him. Photographs taken at the time show him on the tennis court, lobbing the ball across the net, an impish smile on his face. Actually, however, he never learnt to play tennis. At Dorothy's urging, he had taken lessons, but after one set he was disabled for a week and retired from the sport. Similarly, he was photographed painting the bottom of a boat. It was an attractive picture of the great tenor holding a paintbrush, but his brush never touched the boat.

His activities were, instead, sedentary ones. He took time out to spend an afternoon at a Southampton fair, drawing caricatures for the benefit of a local hospital, but he spent most of his time at home, playing with his baby, helping to entertain Dorothy's friends and family, working at his stamp collection (with the help of Mimmi) and preparing himself for his autumn commitments.

In September, Caruso's Long Island holiday came to an end. On the fourteenth of the month, he began three days of recording in Camden, New Jersey. These recordings included the great tenor scene from *La Juive* and the *Crucifixus* from Rossini's *Petite Messe Solennelle*. They were to be of enormous historic significance, the last of the priceless legacy of recordings left by the first great recording artist.

Shortly afterwards, there was yet another American concert tour, one Caruso should never have undertaken; he was still tired and was beginning to show symptoms of what was to become a severe cold. It was an unusually exhausting tour: Caruso not only had to sing, but also had to participate in events which had nothing to do with music. The stops included St Paul, where he spoke at a meeting of the Community Chest; Denver, where he visited the grave of Buffalo Bill outside the city; Tulsa, where he visited the oil fields; Fort Worth, where he found time to examine the local stockyards; and Omaha, where he disappointed his fans by revealing his ignorance of American baseball — when asked what he thought of Babe Ruth, he had to admit that he had never heard 'her' sing. The tour took its toll. When he returned to New York at the end of October, Dorothy was alarmed to find her husband in a state of near exhaustion, both physically and emotionally, and there were only two weeks before he had to begin another long season at the Metropolitan.

21
FAREWELL
to NEW YORK

Though he himself refused to recognize it, Caruso was a sick man at the start of the 1920–21 Metropolitan season. His headaches persisted, and the cold that had plagued him for so long had reached his chest and bones, causing him pain which he tried to conceal from those around him, though several of his friends and associates noted his drawn countenance with dismay. Moreover, his nerves were on edge, and he was frequently ill-tempered. He thought increasingly of retiring from the stage and living out the rest of his life away from the spotlights, in peace and privacy, enjoying the fruits of his many years of hard work.

He opened the Metropolitan season on the night of 15 November, with a performance of *La Juive*; less than six weeks later, on 24 December, he again sang the demanding role in Halévy's opera in what would be the final performance of his extraordinary career. The weeks between these two performances were marred by injuries and illnesses and distinguished by an almost superhuman courage and heroic determination on the part of the tenor whom James Huneker described as not only a great artist, but 'a genuine man'.

The opening performance went well. Though Titta Ruffo, who had been moved to tears by Caruso's performance in the same role the previous year, felt that something was wrong, the press and public agreed that he had succeeded once again in bringing to life the tragic figure of Eléazar, both vocally and dramatically.

His second appearance, a few nights later, in *L'Elisir d'Amore* was not nearly so successful; critics complained that his interpretation lacked 'artistic propriety', and that his treatment of Donizetti's music was 'exaggerated'. But this had nothing to do with any illness — most probably, he was just outgrowing a youthful, light role he had sung so many times in the past. The response to his third appearance, as Samson, was reassuring — those who had criticized his singing a few nights earlier agreed he was in excellent voice — and his performance in *La Juive*, in Philadelphia on 30 November, was also greeted with unanimous praise. In spite of his fatigue, he was continuing to satisfy his public.

His next performance, in New York on the night of 3 December in *Samson et Dalila*, was also acclaimed, but during it he was nearly knocked over when a piece of broken pillar hit him forcefully in the chest. The pain lasted only a short time, and the blow was deemed a trivial one by the physician who examined him and found only a slight bruise. The performance continued in spite of the accident — though physicians later suggested that the apparently trivial blow to his chest might have caused injuries to his pleura and consequently far greater damage than had at first been believed.

Whatever the cause, the accident or a worsening of his cold, Caruso was seized with a chill the following day while out for a drive with Dorothy. He immediately paid a visit to his personal physician, Philip Horowitz, who ordered him to stay in bed.

During the night, the tenor suffered a dull pain in his side, and his cough worsened. He made light of it, refusing further medical attention the following day and insisting that it would pass. In spite of the obvious deterioration of his condition, he was determined to sing a few nights later, on 8 December, in *Pagliacci*. He had a premonition, however, and as he left for the theatre, asked his wife to pray for him.

In spite of what must have been excruciating pain, he began the performance, in which he was joined by his old friends Destinn and De Luca. Towards the end of his great aria, *Vesti la Giubba*, his voice broke on the high A and, to the horror of the audience, he tripped and stumbled off the stage and into the wings.

The public was alarmed, fearing that he might have seriously injured himself in the fall. The truth was far worse. The fall had not been an accident. Caruso, in the middle of his aria, had felt an intense pain in his left side and momentarily blacked out. He had deliberately tripped so that the audience would believe that a minor accident had been the cause of his broken note. Unknown to his public, he had fallen unconscious into the arms of Zirato and had to be carried, helpless, to his dressing room. He was for a moment in a state of panic — gasping and sobbing, fearing that his voice had left him for ever.

He quickly recovered his composure. As he lay in his dressing room, Zirato, Dorothy and his colleagues pleaded with him to terminate the performance, but Dr Horowitz, in attendance, minimized the damage. It was, he assured all, nothing but an attack of intercostal neuralgia. He strapped the tenor to reduce the pain and agreed that he could continue the performance.

The next day, Caruso was still in pain, but he again made light of his problem. He saw no reason not to go on with his regular schedule, preferring to believe the comforting, if implausible, diagnosis of his physician.

The tenor's next performance, in *L'Elisir d'Amore*, was to take place at the Brooklyn Academy of Music on the night of 11 December. In spite of Dr Horowitz's assurances, it turned out to be one of the most dramatic evenings in the history of opera. It began shortly before the curtain was to rise when Caruso, already in costume, started to cough. Upon entering his dressing room, Dorothy found him by the washstand, rinsing his mouth. At first the water he spit into the basin was pink — the result, she believed, of his vigorous brushing of his teeth. It soon turned to red, however, and she realized he was haemorrhaging. She turned to his valet and asked him to summon Dr Horowitz to the theatre, in the meantime pleading with her husband to delay the start of the opera until the doctor's arrival. Caruso stubbornly insisted that the haemorrhage was a minor one and that he would begin to sing as soon as the bleeding stopped.

After applications of ice to the back of his throat, the bleeding did stop, and the performance began. The audience, unaware of the backstage drama, applauded wildly as Caruso, dressed as the innocent, lovesick peasant Nemorino bounded on to the stage. As he began to sing, however, Dorothy, seated in the first row, noticed that his smock was turning red. She watched in horror as her husband repeatedly turned his back to the audience,

coughed and drew a handkerchief from his pocket. In spite of the heavy bleeding, he continued to sing. From time to time, he went towards the wings, where Zirato and stunned members of the chorus passed him towels and handkerchiefs with which he would wipe his mouth. He then discarded them, bloodstained, into a well which was part of the set. Dr Horowitz, who had reached the theatre and was also standing in the wings, vividly described the tenor's remarkably courageous struggle to the New York *Times* a few days later:

> I almost died standing there, watching him. Of course I did not know what was the matter. I could not tell. I had made no examination. No one could tell. I stood there watching him, fighting to go on. You can imagine how I felt! I beckoned, I tried to make him come off the stage, but he paid no attention to me. All the chorus was standing there watching, aghast. Even the musicians, I am told, looked up, wondering whether to go on. Caruso would not stop, so they did go on.

To the astonishment of all those who were aware of his ordeal, Caruso, profusely bleeding yet clear-voiced except for the brief moments when the blood which rushed to his throat threatened to choke him, continued to sing until the close of the act.

When the curtain fell, he was led back to his dressing room, where he was finally convinced that he should not go on with the performance — though he would not actually give up until official word came from Gatti, who was informed of the incident while at his office in New York, authorizing the suspension.

Back in his apartment at the Vanderbilt Hotel, Caruso minimized the importance of the incident. After an examination, Dr Horowitz pronounced that the haemorrhage had been caused by the bursting of a blood vessel at the back of the tenor's tongue, which had worsened as he continued to sing. He informed Gatti, who had rushed to the Vanderbilt to be at his side, that there was no cause for concern. The physician informed the tenor, as he would later inform the press, that the accident was a very slight one, which would in no way prevent Caruso from going on with the season as scheduled.

As if to confirm the doctor's judgement, Caruso sang again only two nights later in *La Forza del Destino*.

THE TENOR was, in his informal photographs, marvellously photogenic. Though he never showed any special interest in photography, in this photograph he seems to be examining a camera with the intensity he usually reserved for his operatic performances.

He sang superbly, and his public was delirious with joy over what seemed to be their hero's complete recovery. The New York critics, too, were relieved. 'No signs of weakness in Caruso's singing,' was the headline in *The World*, and the reviewer for *The American* proclaimed, 'Caruso sings in splendid voice'. A reporter for the *Times* noted that 'Caruso was as frolicsome as a schoolboy and beaming all over his broad countenance with happiness over his complete recovery . . .'

Even the tenor himself seemed to believe what the press had reported. He ordered a telegram to be sent to his son at boarding school, assuring him that all was well, and, elated, dispatched cables to friends around the world, confirming his recovery. To Otto Kahn, he wrote: 'Thanks God it was nothing to be alarmed.'

What Caruso neglected to tell the press or his colleagues was that the pains in his side had not abated, that his successful performance had constituted a courageous victory in a battle against that pain. The same was true three nights later when he masked his pain so skilfully that neither the newspapers nor the audience guessed that his chest had been tightly strapped before the performance by Dr Horowitz and that he had managed to sing only with the greatest of difficulties one of his most demanding roles, that of Samson. 'It was a performance of rare refinement and beauty', according to the *Times*; and 'his superb voice was again in good condition', according to the *Herald*.

In spite of the exhaustion that had overcome him and the agonizing pain he frequently endured, Caruso had sung nine times during the first month of the Metropolitan season. He was proud that none of his appearances had been cancelled — he hated to let his public down; only the Brooklyn *L'Elisir d'Amore* had been suspended, and that under extraordinary circumstances. During the night of 21 December, however, he again suffered excruciating pains in his side. Assured by his doctor the following morning that all was well and that it was no more than another attack of neuralgia, he was determined to sing again in the Donizetti opera that night, but by late afternoon the pains had become so acute that he was forced to agree to a cancellation. It was more important, he reasoned, to rest in order to again sing *La Juive* on Christmas Eve.

That performance was to be his last. Pale and weak, he arrived at the theatre on time as always, determined to prove that he was well. Among those attending the performance was his son Mimmi who had come to New York from the Culver Military Academy in Indiana for the Christmas holidays.

Before the curtain rose, the sixteen-year-old boy went to his father's dressing room, to kiss his hand as was his custom before each performance he attended. He knocked at the door and, after he heard a familiar voice say, 'Avanti', entered the room. In the corner, he saw a stranger, a tall dignified bearded old man. Terrified, he called out, 'Where is my father?' The bearded figure turned towards him; it was his father, who had literally and with enormous effort transformed himself into the character of the elderly goldsmith. Young Caruso kissed his father's hand and returned to his seat.

As the opera was about to begin, Caruso was tightly strapped by the now ever-present Dr Horowitz, who assured him again that his pain was caused by nothing more serious than neuralgia. Nonetheless, the weary tenor implored the soprano Florence Easton to tighten her hold on him, to lessen the pain, while he sang his taxing aria *Rachel! Quand du Seigneur*. The evening proceeded without incident, in spite of Caruso's suffering, though his enormous effort did not go completely unnoticed. Instinctively, he often pressed his hand to his left side in order to relieve the pain, a gesture which troubled at least one member of the audience, the physician of the eminent critic Hermann Klein, who told Klein that Caruso seemed to be in great pain. Toscanini, too, in America on tour, was at the performance and following it expressed his own fears to Gatti. 'The man must be sick,' he told the managing director. 'He looks very bad. I am very anxious about him.'

Removed from his costume, relieved that the performance had come successfully to an end, Caruso returned to his home at the Vanderbilt, where Dorothy had prepared the traditional Christmas Eve feast for the tenor and his friends. He tried his best to join in the festivities but his usual enthusiasm was missing. He was weary, and when his guests had left and it was time to go to bed he admitted to his wife that he still had a pain in his side.

Christmas Day began happily. There was a huge, gaily decorated Christmas tree in the Caruso apartment; underneath it lay enormous piles of gifts for the family, the servants and friends. Caruso had wanted to make this first Christmas for his daughter, who was little more than a year old, an especially joyous one. Under the fireplace was a splendid crib, and on a table was a bag containing the gold pieces to be distributed to the employees of the Metropolitan, as was Caruso's annual custom.

Shortly after noon, while handing out presents to the servants, Caruso felt a sharp and, this time, unfamiliar pain. What followed is best described in a letter written by him to his brother more than a month later:

> I arrived in my bathroom. I began to wash my mouth, but that strange illness took me again and then I decided to throw myself into hot water. I drew a tepid bath and got in, but did not have the time to sit myself down when I doubled over forward like a

dry twig, screaming like a madman. Everyone from the household came running and they pulled me out. They tried to make me stand, but I was bent over holding my left flank with my left hand and was letting out howls like a wounded dog, so loud they heard me on the street from the eighteenth floor and throughout the whole hotel. They made me sit on a chaise-longue where I could stay only on the edge and always bent forward.

My doctor was called by telephone, and he was not at home. The doctor of the hotel was found who, not knowing my illness and not knowing me, did not hazard to give me anything, but it seems that he gave me a palliative until my doctor arrived . . . Returning to my story, my doctor arrived and said as he had said before that it was an intercostal pain and therefore with a sedative it would pass.

Five days I was between life and death because of the stubbornness of that good doctor. Finally, after the second day, my wife, with the help of my Italian friends, who took turns at being on hand, held various consultations. The last doctor said, 'If this man is not operated on in twelve hours he is gone.' Thought was then given to the surgeon. He was found. He had to have the consent of my wife to operate and when he had it he went to work. It was a case of breaking two ribs because they came to the conclusion that I had purulent pleurisy and the fluid had begun to reach the heart. What a mess. I screamed for five days, seated at the edge of my couch day and night. Finally what I remember is this: sounds of instruments being moved and jarred, and then as if they had placed the point of the knife in the spleen, and then great shouts of 'Hurrah'. What happened was that in making the incision to get to the ribs, the pus came out like an explosion striking the doctor, everything, the whole room. There was no need to cut the ribs which would have been painful . . .

Caruso's progress was reported at length in the press each day and, by 31 December the news was encouraging: 'We are not alarmed now, though we know that he is seriously ill,' Zirato told reporters. Later bulletins, too, were optimistic, and by 10 January the tenor's team of physicians were able to announce that the patient was convalescent

CARUSO

and that no further bulletins would be issued. Plans were being made for a visit to Atlantic City, where he was expected to complete his recovery.

In spite of this optimistic prognosis, Caruso's fever returned in early February. Once again, the team of doctors assembled, and a series of operations was decided upon, the most serious involving the removal of four inches of one of his ribs. He had dreaded this possibility and was not informed of it, nor was he told that his left lung had contracted. His suffering was intense, and on the night of 15 February his heart began to fail. Friends, including Scotti, were summoned to bid their final farewells. Two priests arrived late in the night, and the last rites of the church were completed at 1.30 in the morning. An urgent telegram was sent to Mimmi at his school in Indiana, in the hope that he might be able to see his father before what seemed the inevitable end.

Miraculously, Caruso survived the night; by morning he even showed some slight signs of improvement. His overpowering will to live had sustained him, and his physicians, though maintaining that his condition remained critical, cautiously predicted that their patient might soon be out of danger.

With the arrival of his son on the morning of 17th, he seemed to take a decided turn for the better. When the boy had received the telegram urging him to rush to New York, he had been working at the stables of the military school; there had been no time to change his clothing before leaving for New York. He was understandably wary as he approached his father's bed, took his hand and kissed it. Caruso, who had been wavering for hours between consciousness and unconsciousness, opened his eyes and smiled. 'You stink, my son,' he said. It was a turning point in his struggle to survive.

Another visit, too, cheered him that morning, a call paid by the Italian ambassador to the United States who conveyed the prayers and wishes of the King and the people of Italy. Caruso was moved. 'I want to die in Italy,' he told his country's ambassador.

In spite of these encouraging signs, Caruso was not yet out of danger. Further surgery, minor but painful, was performed in his hotel suite, which had been transformed into a miniature hospital, and his fever lingered. His moods alternated between optimism and pessimism. On 26 February, fearing the end might be near, he asked

CARUSO

DURING HIS FINAL ILLNESS, Caruso was treated by a number of doctors in New York. Shown here is the bill sent by one of them, Dr Antonio Stella, who saw the tenor, often several times a day, for six months. Caruso insisted that the $15,850 bill be reduced to $15,000.

to see his Metropolitan colleagues once again to say goodbye, and he was visited by Scotti (who had been a daily caller), Bori, Ponselle, Amato and the young tenor Beniamino Gigli. The latter wrote in his memoirs: 'We stood round his bed, trying desperately to be cheerful, but most of his old friends . . . were unable to restrain their tears.'

Another visitor, Titta Ruffo, who had agreed to sing in *Otello* with Caruso the following season — Caruso's first appearance in the role of the Moor, and a performance which would surely have made operatic history — was shocked by the tenor's appearance. 'His magnificent torso was nothing but a skeleton,' Ruffo noted.

In early March, a few days after his forty-eighth birthday — celebrated quietly and without the usual party — Caruso, who was still weak, was given a blood transfusion, after which he showed slow but steady signs of improvement. Warned that he could not travel to Italy until he was fully recovered, he followed his doctors' orders and kept his activities to a minimum. By mid-April, he was able to write to Puccini in Milan that he was much better and planned to leave for Naples by the end of May.

Before leaving, Caruso visited the Metropolitan to say goodbye to all the workers at the opera house which had been his home for much of his professional life. These employees, among them porters, doormen and cleaning women, did their best to hide their shock at his appearance — he had lost 50 lbs, his skin was pallid, and he was stooped to one side — and congratulated him on his recovery.

Caruso was not fooled, however. Though optimistic that the Italian sun might restore his strength, he knew he was still a very sick man. He was undeniably weak, his shirt collar had become far too large (he joked about this but knew it was no laughing matter), and there was a tingling and numbness in his right hand, a brachial paralysis, the result of lying on his right arm during surgery. Even worse, he learned to his horror shortly before sailing that, as he had feared, a part of his rib had indeed been removed during one of the operations. This unexpected news stunned him: he immediately told Salvatore Fucito, his accompanist, who was packing his scores, that he had decided not to take his music with him to Italy.

214 EAST 16TH STREET
NEW YORK
1921
May 26th

Comm, Enrico Caruso

Vanderbilt Hotel

TO ANTONIO STELLA, M. D.

FOR PROFESSIONAL SERVICES

From
December 26th 20
tp January 19th 21
$ 5.000,00

From
January 20th
to February 3rd
750.00

From February 4th
to March 19th
9000.00

From March 20th
toMay 26th
1100,00

$ 15.850.00

Reduced to $15.000 . ←

RECEIVED PAYMENT

Antonio Stella

STATEMENTS RENDERED MONTHLY
AN ITEMIZED ACCOUNT MAY BE HAD IF DESIRED

Con sentiti ringraziamenti .

22
FINALE

Caruso, his wife and their daughter sailed for Naples on the *SS Presidente Wilson* on 28 May. Thin and weak, he had to be helped on to the ship. The party arrived on 9 June. Caruso was home, greeted by a cheering crowd of his fellow Neapolitans.

After a few days in Naples, where the tenor was reunited with his stepmother and with Fofò, who had come from Florence to meet him, they took the short trip to Sorrento, where they planned to spend two quiet months by the sea before going on to the Villa Bellosguardo. Settled into a luxurious suite in Sorrento's Hotel Vittoria, Caruso led a quiet life. He swam, he sunbathed — he believed the sun and the waters might cure him — and he took short walks. On his infrequent visits to the town, he was greeted with both affection and awe — for the townspeople he was a king who had returned from voluntary exile to his home. Dorothy, aware that his recovery was far from complete, did her best to see that he did not exert himself too much. In spite of this, he insisted upon visiting Capri and, later, Pompeii; both short trips exhausted him.

Visitors, except for close friends like Gatti-Casazza who came to Sorrento in July, were kept away so that Caruso might rest in privacy. Nonetheless, one day he agreed to audition a young Neapolitan singer who had shown the courage to approach him. It proved to be an exhilarating experience. The young man arrived at the hotel with the score of *Martha* in hand. He attempted

THIS IS THE LAST PHOTOGRAPH of Caruso, taken on the balcony of the Hotel Vittoria in Sorrento, on 6 July 1921. The tenor's health was, apparently, improving, but it soon deteriorated, and he died in less than a month.

the popular aria *M'appari* and failed. Caruso stopped him, shouting 'No, no!' and began to sing the aria himself. To his astonishment, his voice was strong and clear. 'Doro,' he called ecstatically to his wife. 'I can sing! I can sing! I have not lost my voice.'

Not since the beginning of his illness had Caruso been so encouraged; if he still had his voice, he was still very much alive. On 17 July, he wrote a cheerful note to Fucito, who had stayed behind in New York. 'I am in good health, thanks to the sun and sea baths,' he wrote. 'I have a voice to sell for another score of years. Whatever I do, I do with great vigour.' Two days later, he told a reporter for the *Chicago Tribune* of his recovery. 'I am gaining strength and weight every day,' he affirmed. 'Those who say I have sung my last on the operatic stage are wrong, for my voice is unimpaired.' When the reporter expressed surprise that he was smoking his customary cigarette, he exclaimed, 'Of course I smoke. What do you think? That I am sick?'

Even while issuing his lighthearted statements, the familiar pains in his side were returning, as was the high fever. For a time he minimized the seriousness of his condition and refused to see any doctor other than the old man who had cared for his mother — the same physician who urged him to spend hours in the polluted waters off Sorrento, while one partially open wound remained on his scarred body. But finally, as his condition worsened, he agreed to allow other doctors to be called in. There were endless consultations, but no decisions were made. No one, it seemed, wanted to make decisions that might possibly lead to the death of the beloved, world-famous singer. Dorothy, frantic, turned to Giuseppe De Luca, who had been visiting his old friend, for advice. The baritone, who had been alarmed by Caruso's rapid deterioration, suggested that the Bastianelli brothers (Giuseppe and Raffaele), considered among the finest doctors in Italy, be summoned from Rome.

The distinguished physicians arrived on the morning of 29 July. After a quick examination, they informed Dorothy that one of the tenor's kidneys had to be removed, and set 3 August as the date for the operation which they insisted had to be performed in Rome. They assured her that the trip would involve no risk, nor would the delay of several days be deleterious.

Later that same day, Caruso wrote to his friend Marziale Sisca. 'Undoubtedly I am passing through an ugly period of convalescence, for I am constantly troubled by acute pains, which worry me.' He told Sisca of the forthcoming trip to Rome, and ended with the encouraging news that the Bastianellis had assured him that he would be able to sing again within four or five months.

The resumption of his work had dominated his thoughts for weeks. Just as he had yearned for Italy while ill in America, while in Sorrento he had looked forward to his return to New York — that, for him, meant a return to the operatic stage, and to his real world. Nevertheless, in spite of the doctors' assurances, he had his doubts, which he expressed in a letter to Gatti-Casazza following the examination by the doctors. His *padrone*, as he liked to call him, had written to ask his ideas concerning the coming opera season, and the tenor had replied that he was not yet in good health and could not say anything. 'The good Lord will do what He wishes,' he concluded.

Caruso wrote no more letters. The following night he became delirious as his temperature rose. In desperation Dorothy called Giovanni in Naples and summoned him to Sorrento at once, asking him to have a private train ready to take her husband from Naples to Rome and to reserve quarters in Naples, where they would spend the night before going on to Rome.

On 31 July, Caruso, Dorothy and Giovanni arrived at the Hotel Vesuvio in Naples where they were joined by Fofò, who had again come from Florence. The following day, the tenor took a serious turn for the worse. It was a day of suffering excruciating pain that none of the many doctors present could alleviate. Their attempts to do so were as clumsy as their diagnoses and treatment had been inept. The unbearable agony continued throughout the night, and by morning, Caruso, short of breath, was only able to moan, '*Calore . . . dolore . . . calore . . . dolore*,' as his helpless family looked on. Shortly after nine o'clock on the morning of 2 August 1921, the suffering came to an end. Enrico Caruso was dead at the age of forty-eight. The cause of his death was peritonitis and sepsis (a bacterial invasion of the body).

Word of his death spread quickly throughout the world. In Europe, Gatti-Casazza learned of it from a newspaper report. He wrote to Otto Kahn: 'We may have now and later tenors possessing some of his qualities, i.e., who may have a beautiful voice, who may be good singers or artists, etc., but I think it will almost be impossible to have the fortune to find again another personality who possesses in himself all the artistic and moral gifts that distinguished our poor and illustrious friend.'

The people of New York, where he had given of himself most generously, were distraught. Vincent Sheean, a prominent American journalist whose personal passion was the opera, remembered many years later: 'The whole city seemed plunged into mourning and actually the words overheard in the streets and in public conveyances were mostly about the departed tenor.'

It was the same elsewhere. Tributes poured in from the tenor's friends, his grateful and appreciative colleagues, and countless others who had never seen him, but whose lives had been enriched by his voice and his singular ability to communicate his joy at the simple fact of being alive.

His funeral was that of a king. The King of Italy gave orders that Naples' Royal Basilica of San Francesco di Paola, reserved for royalty, be used for the services, and the streets of Naples were lined with tearful crowds as the funeral procession moved from a temporary chapel at the Hotel Vesuvio to the church.

THE GREAT TENOR'S FUNERAL at the Royal Basilica of San Francesco di Paola in Naples. It was a day of mourning in many parts of the world.

CARUSO

Caruso's vibrant presence, his immense warmth, and the personal charm that enabled him to touch the hearts of the people had been lost for ever. Nonetheless, through the recordings he left behind, his splendid voice would never be silenced. The first of the recording superstars, his records sold millions of copies while he was alive and have continued to sell steadily since his death. New collections of these recordings, taking advantage of the latest methods of sound reproduction, have been issued periodically in both Europe and the United States; indeed recently RCA Victor (in the United States) have issued a 'complete' Caruso on twelve compact discs.

Seventy years after his death, Caruso remains a unique figure in the history of music, his name synonymous with the glory of the human voice. Other great singers have come and gone, but, while Caruso remains a household name, few are remembered. A search for a 'new Caruso' has proved fruitless. The first tenor to be proclaimed his successor, Beniamino Gigli, most probably summed up the feelings of many artists when, in a letter to the New York *Times*, he wrote:

I believe that to speak of this [a successor to Caruso] is a sacrilege and a profanity to his memory; it means violating a tomb which is sacred to Italy and the entire world. The efforts of every artist today aim to gather and to conserve the artistic heritage received from the great singer, and everyone must strive to do this, not with vain self-advertisement, but with tenacious study for the triumph of the pure and the beautiful. He struggled for this, and we, for the glory of his art, must follow his example with dignity.

CHRONOLOGY

1873:   Enrico Caruso is born in Naples on 25 February, the son of Marcellino Caruso and Anna Baldini.

1883:   Caruso becomes apprentice to a mechanical engineer and, at the same time, begins his studies at the Bronzetti Institute, which specializes in training young boys to sing in church choirs. His teachers discover his extraordinarily rich contralto voice.

1888:   Caruso's mother dies on 1 June, and his father marries Maria Castaldi in November.

1890:   Caruso begins to sing at cafés along the waterfront.

1891:   While continuing with his factory job, Caruso becomes part of the regular entertainment at the well-known Café Risorgimento. There he meets Eduardo Missiano who recognizes his talent and introduces him to Guglielmo Vergine, Caruso's first professional teacher.

1894:   Caruso receives a call-up for three years of military service in Rieti but, with the intervention of Major Nagliati, a music lover, he is discharged after less than two months and replaced by his younger brother Giovanni. Following his return to Naples, he gives up his factory job to devote himself full time to his singing. He auditions for Nicola Daspuro and is hired to sing in *Mignon* at the Teatro Mercadante. However, he performs poorly at the piano rehearsal and is dismissed.

1895:   Caruso makes his professional operatic début on 15 March in Domenico Morelli's *L'Amico Francesco* at the Teatro Nuovo in Naples. The new opera, a failure, is given only two of four scheduled performances.

        Sings in *Cavalleria Rusticana* and *Faust* at the Teatro Cimarosa in Caserta — his first chance to sing in operas which are part of the standard repertory.

Replaces an indisposed tenor at the Teatro Bellini in Naples and performs successfully in *Faust*, *Rigoletto*, and *La Traviata*. Travels to Egypt to sing with an Italian opera company, his first performances for a foreign public. Hired for a long season at the Teatro Mercadante.

1896: Concludes the Mercadante season with a *serata d'onore*, a sign of his success.

Sings in Salerno where he meets Vincenzo Lombardi who becomes his vocal coach and teaches him to sing the difficult tenor role in *I Puritani*.

In the autumn, sings *Pagliacci* for the first time.

1897: Sings in *La Gioconda* at the Teatro Massimo in Palermo. After obtaining Puccini's consent, sings his first Rodolfo in *La Bohème* in Livorno. Falls in love with Ada Giachetti, who sings the role of Mimi. They live together as man and wife, though they never marry.

Makes a very successful début in Milan at the Teatro Lirico in *La Navarraise*. At the Lirico creates the role of Federico in *L'Arlesiana* before an enthusiastic public.

1898: Birth of Caruso's and Giachetti's first son, Rodolfo (Fofò). Enormous success as Loris in *Fedora* at the opera's world première at the Teatro Lirico.

Sings in St Petersburg.

1899: First visit to South America.

Returns to St Petersburg.

Makes début in Rome in *Iris* and not in Puccini's new opera, *Tosca*, as he had hoped.

1900: In poor health makes a disappointing début in *La Bohème* at Milan's La Scala.

1901: First La Scala triumph, in *L'Elisir d'Amore*, in February. In December makes eagerly awaited début at San Carlo in Naples. After a mixed reception, he vows never to sing in Naples again.

1902: In February, sings with Melba for the first time, in *La Bohème* in Monte Carlo.

In April, makes his first recordings in Milan.

In May, triumphant début at Covent Garden in *Rigoletto*.

1903: In November, début at the Metropolitan Opera House in *Rigoletto*.

1904: Caruso, the international star, sings in Monte Carlo, Paris, Barcelona, Prague, Berlin and London.

First full season at the Metropolitan Opera House in New York and tours America.

Buys Villa Bellosguardo near Florence.

Birth of second son, Enrico Caruso, Jr (Mimmi).

1906: Caruso in San Francisco with the Metropolitan Opera Company during earthquake. Monkey House case.

1908: At the Metropolitan, Caruso sings Manrico in *Il Trovatore* for the first time.
Death of his father.
Ada Giachetti leaves him for the family chauffeur.

1909: Caruso, in poor health, operated on in Milan for a throat ailment.

1910: Threatened by the Black Hand.
In December, creates the role of Dick Johnson in Puccini's *La Fanciulla del West* at the Metropolitan.

1911: Illness forces Caruso to leave the Metropolitan in February, cancelling the rest of his engagements there.
In September, apparently in good health, returns to the stage in Vienna.

1912: Giachetti on trial in Milan for defamation of character.

1913: Caruso returns to Covent Garden for the first time in many years.

1914: Last performance in London. Sings in Rome, the first time in Italy for more than ten years.

1915: South American tour.
In September, sings *Pagliacci* in Milan, his farewell to the Italian public.
Emergence as a true dramatic tenor at Metropolitan opening in *Samson et Dalila*.

1917: Final tour of South America.

1918: Sings in *Le Prophète* at the Metropolitan in February.
Makes two films in New York.
Marries Dorothy Park Benjamin on 21 August.

1919: Spends summer at Bellosguardo with Dorothy and his two sons.
Sings in Mexico. On 22 November, triumphs as Eléazar in *La Juive* at the Metropolitan.
First daughter, Gloria, born in December.

1920: Sings in Cuba. Makes his last recording in September.
On 11 December, during a performance of *L'Elisir d'Amore* in Brooklyn, suffers a haemorrhage and the performance is suspended.
On 24 December, sings in *La Juive* at the Metropolitan — his final performance.

1921: Caruso, a sick man, returns to Italy in June. In Sorrento his health seems to improve, but it worsens in July, and he is brought to the Hotel Vesuvio in Naples where he dies on the morning of 2 August.

SELECT
BIBLIOGRAPHY

Aldrich, Richard. *Concert Life in New York (1902–1923).* New York: Putnam, 1941.

Barblan, Guglielmo. *Toscanini e la Scala.* Milan: Edizioni della Scala, 1972.

Barthélemy, Richard. *Memories of Caruso,* trans. Constance Camner. Plainsboro, N.J.: La Scala Autographs, 1979.

Bello, John. *Enrico Caruso, a Centennial Tribute.* Providence: Universal Associates, 1973.

Bernays, Edward L. *Biography of an Idea.* New York: Simon and Schuster, 1965.

Bolig, John Richard. *The Recordings of Enrico Caruso.* Dover: The Eldridge Reeves Johnson Memorial, Delaware State Museum, 1973.

Bracale, Adolfo. *Mis Memorias.* Caracas: Editorial Elite, 1931.

Burke, Billie, and Shipp, Cameron. *With a Feather on My Nose.* London: Peter Davies, 1950.

Calvé, Emma. *My Life.* London: Appleton, 1922.

Cambiasi, Pompeo. *La Scala 1778–1906.* Milan: Ricordi, 1908.

Camner, James. *How to Enjoy Opera.* New York: Doubleday, 1981.

Caruso, Dorothy. *Enrico Caruso, His Life and Death.* London: T. Werner Laurie, 1946.

Caruso, Dorothy, and Goddard, Terrance. *Wings of Song, the Story of Caruso.* London: Hutchinson, 1928.

Caruso, Enrico. *Caruso's Caricatures.* London: Constable, 1977.

Colson, Percy. *Melba: An Unconventional Biography.* London: Grayson and Grayson, 1932.

Crabbé, Armand. *L'Art d'Orphée.* Brussels: Editions Inter-nos, 1946.

Daspuro, Nicola. *Enrico Caruso.* Mexico: Ediciones Coli, 1943.

Farrar, Geraldine. *Geraldine Farrar.* Boston: Houghton Mifflin, 1916.

Farrar, Geraldine. *Such Sweet Compulsion.* New York: Greystone Press, 1938.

Freestone, J., and Drummond, H.J. *Enrico Caruso, His Recorded Legacy.* London: Sidgwick and Jackson, 1960.

Gaisberg, Fred. *The Music Goes Round.* New York: Macmillan, 1942.

Gara, Eugenio. *Caruso, Storia di un emigrante.* Milan: Rizzoli, 1947.

Gatti, Carlo. *Il Teatro alla Scala.* Milan: Ricordi, 1964.

Gatti-Casazza, Giulio. *Memories of the Opera.* London: John Calder, 1977.

Gelatt, Roland. *The Fabulous Phonograph.* London: Cassell, 1956.

Hempel, Frieda. *Mein Leben dem Gesang.* Berlin: Argon Verlag, 1955.

Hetherington, John. *Melba.* London: Faber and Faber, 1961.

Key, Pierre V.R., with Zirato, Bruno. *Enrico Caruso.* London: Hurst & Blackett, 1923.

Klein, Hermann. *The Golden Age of Opera.* London: Routledge, 1933.

Kolodin, Irving. *The Metropolitan Opera, 1883–1939.* New York: Oxford University Press, 1940.

Ledner, Emil. *Erinnerungen an Caruso.* Hannover: P. Steegemann, 1922.

McCormack, John. *John McCormack, His Own Life Story,* transcribed by Pierre V.R. Key, ed. by John Scarry. New York: Vienna House, 1973.

Maria y Campos, Armando de. *El Canto del Cisne (Una temporada de Caruso en Mexico).* Mexico: Editorial Telón, 1952.

Matz, Mary Jane. *The Many Lives of Otto Kahn.* New York: Macmillan, 1963.

Melba, Nellie. *Melodies and Memories.* London: Butterworth, 1925.

Moses, Montrose J. *The Life of Heinrich Conried.* New York: Crowell, 1916.

Petriccione, Diego. *Caruso nell'arte e nella vita.* Naples: Santojanni, 1939.

Pituello, Luciano. *Caruso a Milano.* Milan: Associazione amici del Museo Teatrale alla Scala, 1971.

Pleasants, Henry. *The Great Singers.* London: Simon and Schuster, 1967.

Robinson, Francis. *Caruso, His Life in Pictures.* London: Thames & Hudson, 1958.

Rosenthal, Harold. *Two Centuries of Opera at Covent Garden.* London: Putnam, 1958.

Ruffo, Titta. *La Mia Parabola.* Rome: Staderini, 1977.

Schoen-Rene, Anna Eugenie. *America's Musical Inheritance.* New York: Putnam, 1941.

Seligman, Vincent. *Puccini among Friends.* London: Macmillan, 1938.

Seltsam, William. *Metropolitan Opera Annals.* New York: Wilson, 1947.

Tetrazzini, Luisa, and Caruso, Enrico. *The Art of Singing.* New York: The Metropolitan Company, 1909.

Thomas, Gordon, and Witts, Max Morgan. *The San Francisco Earthquake.* New York: Stein and Day, 1971.

Timberlake, Craig. *The Bishop of Broadway.* New York: Library Publishers, 1954.

Ybarra, T.R. *Caruso, the Man of Naples and the Voice of Gold.* London: Cresset Press, 1954.

INDEX

Numbers in *italics* refer to captions of illustrations

INDEX

ACKNOWLEDGEMENTS

Author's Acknowledgements

I have spent many years studying the life and work of Enrico Caruso, and during those years I have been helped by very many people . . . far too many to mention here.

However, for special help in preparing and writing this volume, I would like to acknowledge my indebtedness to the following: Jean Bowen of the Library for the Performing Arts in New York and Edwin A. Quist and Elizabeth Schaaf of the Peabody Institute in Baltimore, who facilitated my researches; Joseph Lewis, who brought interesting new material to my attention; Gwyn Hughes Jones, who enabled me 'to see' Caruso and thus enriched my perception of the tenor and his world; Dr Adrian Zorgniotti, who furnished me with valuable information concerning Caruso's illness and death; and James Camner, who was as always unfailingly generous in sharing his vast knowledge and understanding of the world of opera and of the musical theatre.

Above all, warm acknowledgement and gratitude are due to Anna Williams, who brought together and selected the illustrations used in this volume. She did far more than that and proved to be the ideal collaborator. I was most fortunate to have the opportunity to work with her and welcome this chance to thank her for all she has done.

Illustration Acknowledgements

Title page Stuart-Liff Collection; 6 Gloria Caruso; 8 Museo Teatrale alla Scala; 10, 11 Gloria Caruso; 12 The Hulton Picture Company; 13 Pierre Key; 14 John Bello Collection; 17 Museo Teatrale alla Scala; 18 Royal Opera House Archives; 20 Jillian Duffy; 23 Museo Teatrale alla Scala; 24 Stuart-Liff Collection; 27, 28 Metropolitan Opera; 30 Royal Opera House Archives; 31 Pierre Key; 32 John Bello Collection; 34 James Camner; 36 Stuart-Liff Collection; 37 Royal Opera House Archives; 38 Stuart-Liff Collection; 39 The Hulton Picture Company; 41 Michael Sisca; 42, 44 Metropolitan Opera; 46 The Hulton Picture Company; 48 EMI Archives; 49, 51 Royal Opera House Archives; 52 Stuart-Liff Collection; 53 The Hulton Picture Company; 54, 57, 59 Metropolitan Opera; 61 John Bello Collection; 62 Metropolitan Opera; 64 and running heads Royal Opera House Archives; 66, 67 by permission of the McCormack family; 70 OPUS 30; 72 Stuart-Liff Collection; 73 The Hulton Picture Company; 77 The Billy Rose Theatre Collection, New York Public Library at Lincoln Centre, Astor, Lenox and Tilden Foundations; 78 Museo Teatrale alla Scala; 82, 83 The Billy Rose Theatre Collection, New York Public Library; 87, 88 Stuart-Liff Collection; 89 Royal Opera House Archives; 92 James Camner; 95 Royal Opera House Archives; 98 The Billy Rose Theatre Collection, New York Public Library at Lincoln Centre, Astor, Lenox and Tilden Foundations; 102, 106 Museo Teatrale alla Scala; 108 Metropolitan Opera; 116 Michael Sisca; 118 Royal Opera House Archives; 120 Culver Pictures; 123 Royal Opera House Archives; 126 James Camner; 128, 131 Metropolitan Opera; 135 Culver Pictures; 136 Museo Teatrale alla Scala; 139 Stuart-Liff Collection; 147 Culver Pictures; 149 James Camner; 151 Metropolitan Opera; 154 Museo Teatrale alla Scala; 156 Metropolitan Opera; 159 James Camner; 160 Archives of the Peabody Institute; 161 courtesy BMG Classics; 163 James Camner; 168 Stuart-Liff Collection; 173 James Camner; 175 Dr Adrian Zorgniotti; 176 James Camner; 180, 181 Museo Teatrale alla Scala.